Me and my Horse

Toni Webber

COPPER BEECH BOOKS
Brookfield, Connecticut

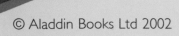

© Aladdin Books Ltd 2002

Produced by:
Aladdin Books Ltd
28 Percy Street
London W1T 2BZ

ISBN 0–7613–1633–7

*First published in the United States
in 2002 by:*
Copper Beech Books,
an imprint of
The Millbrook Press
2 Old New Milford Road
Brookfield, Connecticut 06804

Editor:
Harriet Brown

Designers:
Flick, Book Design & Graphics
Simon Morse

Illustrators:
Peter Barrett, McRae Books—Italy,
David Burroughs, Donald Harley—
BL Kearley, James Field, Terry Riley,
Chris Tomlin, Stephen Sweet, Ross
Watton—SGA, Steve Roberts—Wildlife
Art Agency, Angus McBride,
Simon Morse, Richard Orr, Francis
Phillipps, Rob Shone, Frederick St Ward

Cartoons: Simon Morse

Picture researcher: Brian Hunter Smart

Certain illustrations have
appeared in earlier books
created by Aladdin Books.

Printed in U.A.E.

Cataloging-in-Publication data
is on file at the Library of Congress

10 9 8 7 6 5 4 3 2 1

Contents

Introduction

Me and My Horse is a lively guide which provides the information you need to help you get the most out of horses and riding. There are always new things to learn and new activities to try with your horse. This book will help you learn to ride, care for your horse, and go on to more advanced activities like show jumping, cross-country, and dressage. Find out more about the amazing world of horses, enjoy spending time with your horse, make friends, and above all, have fun!

Follow Oscar and me as we learn to ride and have fun together —and do our best not to get into too much trouble!

Always Remember:
Look in these boxes for further information about horses and riding. They contain important points that you should try to remember.

✓ **THE RIGHTS AND WRONGS**
Watch for these check boxes, as they show you how to do things correctly. Just as importantly, watch for the "X" boxes. These show you how not to do things. ✗

Follow my horse diary to find out about my riding progress —it could be a lot like yours! Why not make your own horse diary to keep track of your riding skills? It could help you remember all the fun you have with horses and new friends as you learn to ride.

Q What are these boxes for?

A These question and answer panels are here to help answer any questions you may have about horses and riding. They are on subjects relevant to the rest of the page they're on.

CHAPTER 1
Learning to ride

In the past, horses were used as a form of transportation, to deliver messages, and to pull plows and carts. Today, hundreds of thousands of people all over the world enjoy riding horses and ponies. As you learn to ride you will make friends, have fun, and get to explore the countryside around you.

YOU AND YOUR HORSE

Horses and ponies are beautiful creatures. If they are well cared for they can give you affection, loyalty, fun, and excitement.

Q I want to learn to ride. Where can I find someone to teach me?

A In the U.S., most riding schools have some sort of official approval, which you should always look out for. Your local Pony Club or your town recreation office may be able to recommend a good riding school. If you see children in riding clothes, stop and ask where they ride. Even if they have their own horses, there may be someone there who is qualified to teach you.

Q Do horses make friends with each other and with people?

A Horses are herd animals and can form strong bonds with each other. They groom one another as a mother would groom her foal. You can make friends with your horse. As you get to know each other over time you can build a special, trusting relationship.

TRAINING

Training a horse to carry a rider used to be called "breaking in." Sometimes that meant literally breaking its spirit so that it was too scared to be anything other than obedient. Today, we know that to train a horse and to enjoy riding, you must trust each other.

Saturday

Woke up really early this morning because I was so excited to be going for my first riding lesson. It has taken ages to persuade Mom that this was all I have ever wanted to do. I was nervous to start with. They put me on a pony called Oscar, who is really beautiful. It was great—the instructor said I had a "natural seat!"

MAKING FRIENDS

One of the great things about riding is making friends. If you go to a riding stable, there are likely to be others of your age also learning to ride. At some riding stables you can get free lessons in return for helping out. Some people even spend the whole school vacation helping out at the stable.

Sunday
My instructor asked me if I wanted to help her get Oscar from the field before my lesson. He was miles away in the far corner. I walked straight toward him and just as I got near, he ran off in the other direction! I think I must have scared him.

Horse sense

Horses like company. In a field they will happily live with horses or other grazing animals, such as sheep, cows, or goats. They communicate using body language and facial expressions. By watching a horse, you can learn to understand what it is thinking.

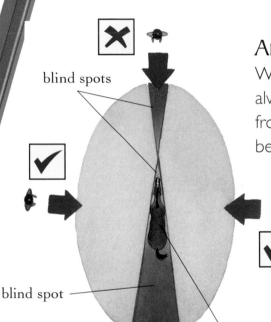

blind spots

blind spot

horse

APPROACHING YOUR HORSE

When you go up to a horse, always approach from the front and at an angle. This is because a horse's eyes are positioned so that it cannot see anything directly in front or behind. Talk to your horse as you approach.

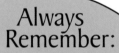

Always Remember:

Be careful when handling sensitive areas. The belly can be a ticklish spot, and you should only use a soft body brush to remove mud and dirt. Clean the eyes and nostrils with a sponge that has been rinsed out in clean water. Use a separate sponge for cleaning the dock area (under the tail).

PICKING UP LEGS

Stand at a right angle to the horse, and run your hand down the back of the leg. Lean your body against the horse to encourage it to shift its weight onto the other leg. When your hand reaches the fetlock (just above the hoof), pull the foot up. Support the hoof in the palm of your hand.

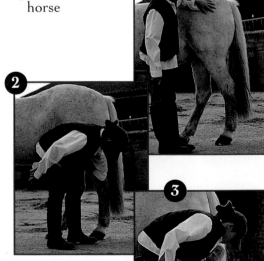

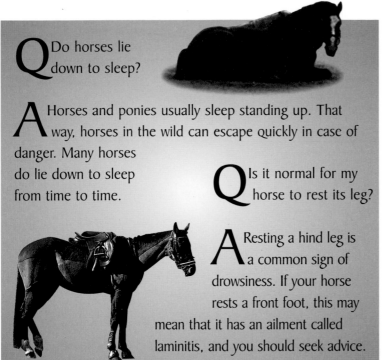

Q Do horses lie down to sleep?

A Horses and ponies usually sleep standing up. That way, horses in the wild can escape quickly in case of danger. Many horses do lie down to sleep from time to time.

Q Is it normal for my horse to rest its leg?

A Resting a hind leg is a common sign of drowsiness. If your horse rests a front foot, this may mean that it has an ailment called laminitis, and you should seek advice.

Attention
This horse is alert. Both ears are pointed forward in the same direction.

Contentment
The ears are relaxed and are neither forward nor back. The eyelids may droop and the mouth is relaxed.

HORSE BODY LANGUAGE

When your horse is interested in something, it arches its neck, pricks up its ears, and snorts. If your horse is warning you not to come too close, it may turn its rump toward you. Watching horses closely will help you to understand their language.

Anger
The ears are laid flat back, the nostrils are flared, and the mouth is open, ready to bite.

Fear
The ears are back, the eyes are rolled back to show a lot of white, and the nostrils are flared.

Later
My instructor said that next time I try to catch Oscar in the field I should watch his ears. Apparently they can tell you a lot about how he is feeling. I'll definitely make sure I talk to him as well so that he knows I'm there—I don't want him running off again!

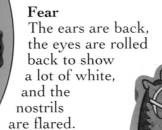

7

Clothing

The two most important items of riding clothing are your hat and your boots. The hat must meet safety requirements and the boots must have a small heel. Warmth and comfort are very important. If you are likely to be riding on the road, you should make sure that you can be seen easily. You do not have to wear a formal riding jacket except on special occasions, but try to look as neatly dressed as you can.

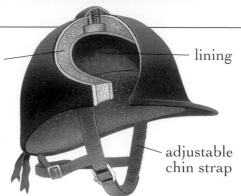

absorbent padding

lining

adjustable chin strap

YOUR RIDING HAT

Hats are either velvet covered with a built-in peak, or a helmet without a peak. These helmets are often covered with a black or colored silk. Both types have straps that fasten under your chin. Get an expert to make sure your hat is a good fit. Always ride with your chin strap fastened.

BE SEEN!

You should always wear light or brightly colored clothing when riding on the road in daylight. At dusk or in the early morning, reflective clothing is essential. It is a good idea for your horse to wear a fluorescent exercise rug, boots, and bandages.

Oscar

Sunday
It was very windy and rainy today. I thought we would stay in the school, but they said we could go for a hack. Luckily I had my new wax riding coat—and so I stayed really dry—and Oscar had his fluorescent exercise rug so we showed up really well.

THE RIGHT GEAR

This rider is dressed for a formal riding occasion. She is wearing jodhpurs, jodhpur boots, shirt, jacket, and most importantly, a riding hat.

hat

jacket

JODHPURS

Jodhpurs are stretchy, to let you move easily and are padded at the knee, to stop rubbing. They come in lots of colors, but beige and gray are most commonly used when dressing for shows.

jodhpurs

jodhpur boots

BOOTS

All riding boots should have a smooth sole and a small, defined heel. Jodhpur boots are short and made of brown or black leather. They reach to just above the ankle. An elastic insert makes them easy to get on and off. Knee-length riding boots are mainly used for special occasions.

Mustn't forget to clean my riding coat and jodhpurs tonight —or Mom will go crazy —they have horse hair all over them!

THE WRONG GEAR

This girl would be unsafe out riding. Rubber boots have ridged soles and her feet could get stuck in the stirrups if she fell. A cap won't protect her head.

GLOVES

Riding gloves have grips on the palms and fingers. The gloves help stop your fingers from slipping on wet reins and keep your hands warm in winter.

Always Remember:

Cover up well in wet and windy weather. Some riding coats have a hood that fits over your riding hat and a skirt big enough to spread out behind you. This is held in place by straps that go under your thighs. These help to stop it from flapping around and startling your horse.
If you want to protect your horse, you could use a waterproof exercise rug.

Getting on and off

pommel

Before you go riding, you have to get on your horse, and when you have finished, you have to get off. This sounds very obvious, but there are ways of doing both that are safe for you and comfortable for your horse. Soon you will be able do both without even thinking about it.

1 Stand at your horse's near (left) side, by its shoulder, and face the rear. Pick up the reins in your left hand and hold the pommel. Put your left foot into the stirrup iron.

STIRRUP LEATHER LENGTH

Make a fist and place your knuckles against the stirrup bar. If the leathers are the right length, the bottom of the iron should reach your armpit.

2 Hold the cantle (back) of the saddle and spring upward. Swing your right leg over the back of the saddle.

3 Lower yourself gently into the saddle, and find the right stirrup with your right foot. Take the reins in both hands and check that your girth is tight.

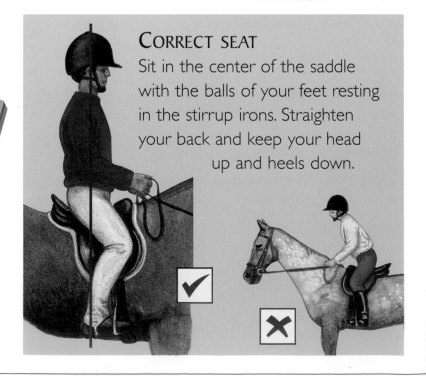

cantle

girth

6 pm

My friend Annabel and I were fooling around today. First, we shortened our stirrups and pretended we were riding in the Kentucky Derby, and then we lengthened them so that we looked like knights of old. We didn't have much control either way. It's a good thing our ponies are so good.

CORRECT SEAT

Sit in the center of the saddle with the balls of your feet resting in the stirrup irons. Straighten your back and keep your head up and heels down.

HOLDING THE REINS AND THE WHIP

The rein should pass between your third finger and little finger of each hand. Your thumb should be on top of the rein. The loop of slack rein hangs down the horse's left shoulder. It is sometimes useful to be able to ride one-handed. To do this with your left hand, for example, take the other rein in that hand and let it pass between your index and middle fingers (see left).

The rider in this picture (left) is holding the reins incorrectly and has little control.

This rider (right) is holding the reins correctly. He can send instant messages to the horse by moving his wrist and tightening his fingers.

To hold a whip correctly, grip it lightly near the top with the lower part of it resting against your thigh (right).

Q Should my stirrups be the same length for all kinds of riding?

A No. When jumping, it is best to shorten your leathers by one or two holes. This will improve your jumping position. It is also a good idea to change your leathers from side to side occasionally. This gives your leathers a chance to stretch evenly as most riders ride more heavily on one side than the other.

4 To get off, wait until your horse is standing still. Hold the reins taut to keep a contact with its mouth, and remove both feet from the stirrups. Hold the pommel with your right hand.

6 Land lightly on both feet. Turn to face the front and be ready to stop your horse from moving on by placing your right hand on the rein.

5 Lean forward slightly and swing your right leg back and over the saddle. Support yourself on your tummy and right hand.

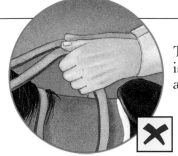

I tried vaulting onto Oscar like they do in mounted games. I thought it would save a lot of time but I was hopeless!

Exercises

Riding is all about balance, suppleness, and flexibility. When you ride, you use muscles that are not otherwise often used. You can develop your muscles by doing exercises. This will give you more control over your body and you won't ache as much.

ARM CIRCLING

Take your feet out of the stirrups and swing one arm in a wide circle, six times in one direction and six in the other. Then repeat the exercise with your other arm.

BACKWARD AND FORWARD

Keep your arms at your sides and lie back until your head is on your horse's rump. Then, fold forward so that your nose is near your horse's neck. Each time, return to the sitting position without using your arms to help you.

HEAD EXERCISES

Neck muscles can get very tired. You can tone them up by rotating your neck in a figure-eight movement. Do this about eight times. Never continue any exercise for too long. A short but regular session is best.

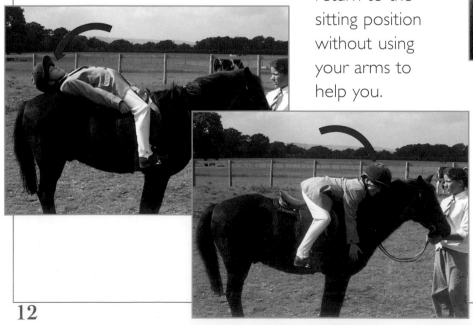

TOUCH TOES

Keeping one arm straight, raise it above your head. Bend at the waist and touch your toes on the opposite side with the tips of your fingers. Do the same with the other arm. This will help to make your body supple.

AROUND THE WORLD

This is a popular exercise for new riders; it helps to improve your balance. There should always be someone on foot, holding the horse when you are doing the exercise.

Always Remember:

Keep your exercising session quite short. It is very easy to pull a muscle when you should be toning it. Some exercises can be done without assistance—such as head and arm circling—but if you are planning to try out "Around the World" you must have someone with you to hold the horse. And, of course, always keep your hat on.

1 Take your feet out of your stirrups and drop the reins. Swing one leg over the horse's neck so that you are sitting sideways.

2 Now swing the other leg over the horse's rump so that you are facing backward. Be careful not to kick the horse with your heel.

3 Continue "Around the World" until you end up in your original position. With practice, you will be able to carry out the whole exercise very quickly.

I was busy touching my toes this morning when Oscar put his head down—I fell off! That makes twice in one week!

The aids

A rider communicates with her horse using natural and sometimes artificial aids. The natural aids are the voice, body, legs, and hands. The artificial ones are the whip, spurs, and martingale. Stick to the natural aids to begin with and introduce the artificial ones as you become more experienced.

BODY, LEGS, AND HANDS

The body really means your body weight. It is an effective aid when used properly. Novice riders should not try to use their body weight as a signal until they can keep perfectly still in the saddle. Legs and hands are also extremely important. Your hands communicate directly with the horse's mouth, and your legs tell your horse whether you want it to turn right or left, go faster, slow down, or stop.

Outside leg
When moving in a straight line, your legs should be at the horse's sides with a gentle but even contact. When turning a corner, your outside leg should apply pressure behind the girth.

girth

Inside leg
The main function of your inside leg is to apply pressure to make your horse move forward. Apply extra pressure when you make a turn so that your horse bends his whole body.

Inside rein
Your hands keep contact with the horse's mouth at all times, and should follow the natural movement of the horse's head. Pressure on the inside rein shows the direction in which you want the horse to go. "Changing the rein" means changing direction.

✗

There was an awful girl in my riding lesson today. She was just dragging poor Pedro around the ring. He was not happy!

VOICE CONTROLS

Always use your voice to give simple commands, whether you are riding or leading your horse. "Walk on" and "halt" are used everywhere, and your horse will quickly learn them.

SPURS

Spurs are used to reinforce the leg aids, but they should be used only by experienced riders. They should be blunt and made of metal.

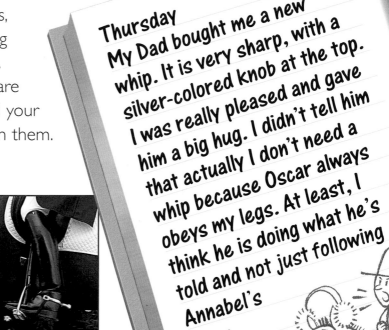

Thursday
My Dad bought me a new whip. It is very sharp, with a silver-colored knob at the top. I was really pleased and gave him a big hug. I didn't tell him that actually I don't need a whip because Oscar always obeys my legs. At least, I think he is doing what he's told and not just following Annabel's pony.

Always Remember:

Carry your whip in your inside hand when riding around a school (arena). You should transfer it to your other hand when changing the rein (changing direction). It is the most important of the artificial aids and the one most usually used by a beginner. Its purpose is to reinforce the leg aids, and you should only use it when your horse doesn't respond to your leg.

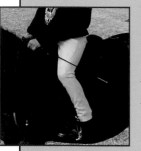

running martingale

standing martingale

MARTINGALES

Both running and standing martingales are used to stop a horse carrying its head too high. They should be fitted so that they only have an effect when the horse raises its head to an angle at which you can't control it. Martingales must not be too short, as this can bruise the horse's mouth.

The gaits

Horses and ponies have four distinct gaits: walk, trot, canter, and gallop. At each gait, the rider's position is slightly different. Whatever your horse is doing and however fast it is traveling, you should keep your body relaxed and your joints supple. If you are stiff or tense, both you and your horse will feel uncomfortable.

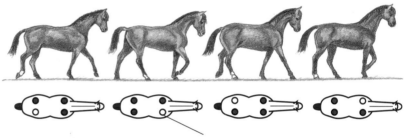

leg off the ground

THE WALK

The walk is a four-beat gait and the feet hit the ground in a regular order. You can count the footfalls—one-two-three-four. Your body should stay still except for a slight movement at your hip and waist. The horse nods its head in the walk, and your hands should "give" with the movement.

Always Remember:

Change the diagonal from time to time when you are doing the rising trot. This means staying in the saddle for one beat so that if you have been rising on the right diagonal you are now rising on the left. This can prevent your horse from becoming stiff on one side. In a ring, you usually change the diagonal when you change the rein. Changing the diagonal is just as important when hacking.

WALK TO TROT

Squeeze your inside leg on the girth, and your outside leg behind the girth. Sit well down in the saddle on your seat bones, and let your hands "give" to allow your horse to move into trot.

Q Do you have to go up and down when you trot?

A No, the sitting trot is often used to improve a rider's position in the saddle. It means exactly what it says—you do not try to rise to the trot at all. You should only do this for short periods.

THE TROT

The trot is a two-beat gait and the horse's feet come down in diagonal pairs. If the trot is energetic, there is a moment when all four feet are off the ground together. Once you learn to rise in the stirrups and sit back in the saddle in rhythm with the horse's movement, you will find it much more comfortable.

There's a new horse in the yard. Its owner does a lot of dressage, and some people think they are good enough for the national team. I watched them schooling this morning and was very impressed. I never realized there were so many different types of trot—working (which I suppose is what Oscar and I do all the time), collected, medium, and extended. Perhaps Oscar and I should be a bit more ambitious!

Down
The rider sits down in the saddle as the horse is on the left diagonal —the near foreleg and the off hindleg are on the ground at the same time.

Up
The rider comes out of the saddle as the horse's off foreleg and near hindleg touch the ground—the right diagonal.

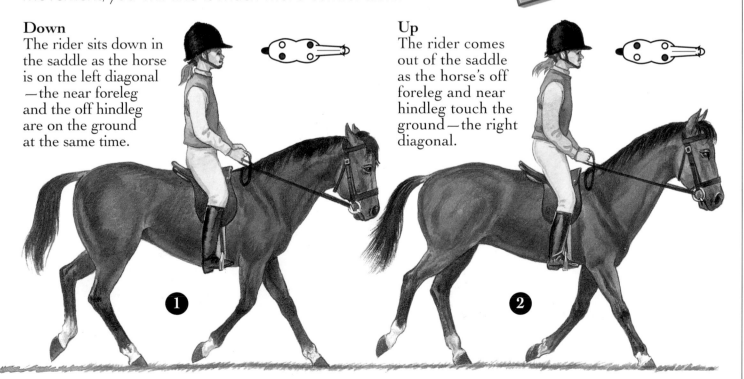

❶

❷

THE CANTER

The canter is a three-beat gait. To keep a proper balance and rhythm when cantering in a circle, your horse should always lead with the inside leg. This horse is leading with its off-foreleg on the right rein.

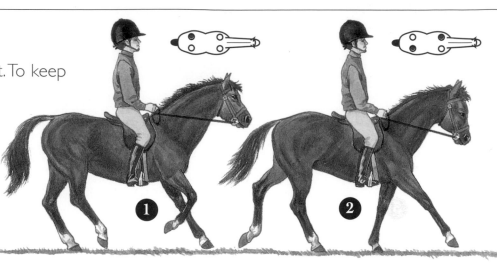

6 pm
We went out on my favorite ride today. It goes up a hill that we all call the Galloping Slope. It's a long grassy track that's flat to start with and then gets steeper. All the ponies know it and as soon as we get to the start, they're off!

TROT TO CANTER

To urge your horse into a canter, stop rising at the trot, sit down, and give the correct aids—inside leg pressure on the girth and outside leg pressure behind the girth.

You will find it easier to make the transition from trot to canter when you're on a bend. This also encourages the horse to strike off with the correct leading leg. At the canter, you should sit well down in the saddle for all three beats. Keep your hips supple and let your body move in rhythm with your horse. Don't lean back as you go into the canter or you could fall off.

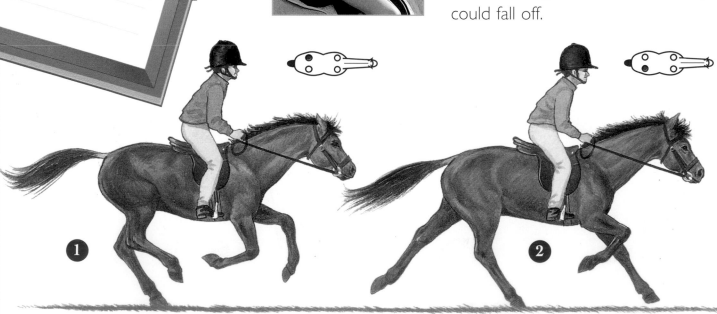

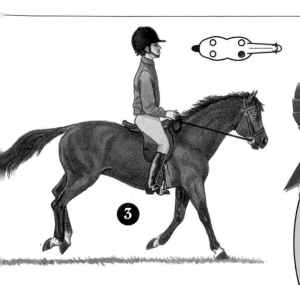

3

Always Remember:

Check that your horse is cantering with the correct leg leading. To begin with, you may have to check by looking down, but as you get more experienced, you will be able to tell by the balance and rhythm of your horse. If you're on the wrong lead, go back to a trot, wait for the next bend, and ask again. Try to concentrate on giving the right aids.

CANTER TO GALLOP

Gallop is a four-beat gait. To make it easier and less tiring for your horse, you should move your weight forward. Shift your weight on your knees and stirrups, and shorten your reins slightly to keep contact with your horse's mouth. Try to keep a straight line from your elbow, through your hand to the bit. Horses can get quite excited when they gallop, so you must be careful not to let the pace get out of hand.

Q Help! How do I slow down?

A To make the transition from a fast pace to a slower one, sit down in the saddle, increase the pressure of your lower legs, and at the same time apply additional pressure on the reins. The rider in the photo (above) is trying to slow down incorrectly and is not using his aids properly. Your horse should stay balanced and the transition should be smooth. In an emergency, turn your horse in an ever-decreasing circle until it is forced to slow down.

Gallop
In a gallop (below left to right) the rider's weight moves forward and is no longer in the saddle. Shortening your stirrup leathers can help you to balance. Your hands should move farther up the horse's neck and "give" with your horse's movement.

3

4

Schooling

The most important part of riding is schooling, or flatwork. When you train your horse to be balanced, flexible, and obedient, all your riding activities will improve. Half an hour of schooling on a regular basis will do wonders for any horse.

FLATWORK

It is safest for both you and your horse if schooling is carried out in an indoor ring. The idea is to get your horse moving rhythmically and in balance. It should carry its head in a natural position, have its weight correctly distributed, be energetic, and give an overall impression of balance and relaxation.

Circles
Circles are a useful way of assessing the flexibility and balance of a horse. In a standard ring (131 feet by 66 feet), ride a circle using half the ring. Your horse's body should follow the curve of the circle.

Serpentine
Gradually introduce serpentine movements, which test and improve the suppleness of your horse. Always keep your inside leg on the girth and your outside leg behind the girth to keep up the tempo of the movements.

Other figures
Smaller figures, such as those shown above, require greater flexibility. Your hips should be parallel with the horse's hindquarters, and your shoulders with the horse's shoulders.

LONGE TRAINING

This has two purposes. One is to exercise your horse if, for any reason, it cannot be ridden. The other is as part of its training. Longeing must be carried out correctly and should not be attempted by an inexperienced person except under strict supervision. If you are longeing, you stand in the center of a circle while the horse moves around you. You control your horse with your voice, a long longe line, which is attached to a longeing noseband on the horse's head, and a long longeing whip.

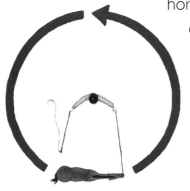

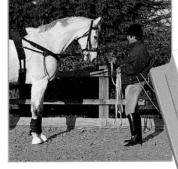

2 + 2 = 4

TROTTING POLES

These are useful when introducing your horse to jumping. They help to develop balance and rhythm, obedience, concentration, and coordination. Jumping poles make good trotting poles, because they are heavy enough not to roll if your horse touches them. The poles should be placed about 4 $\frac{1}{2}$ feet (135 cm) apart, or 3 ft 3 in (100 cm) if your horse is very small.

Always Remember:

Use all the aids when schooling. Many inexperienced riders forget that the voice is an important tool in training a horse. The only time that you are not allowed to use your voice is when you are doing a dressage test. Otherwise, the voice is excellent for calming an excited or nervous horse, and for giving orders.

Walking over poles
Start by showing your horse the poles to reassure it that they are nothing to be afraid of. After a while, it will walk quite happily beside you over the poles.

Riding over poles
Try to be relaxed when riding over trotting poles. Sit straight in the saddle and don't look down or hurry.

Jumping

All horses can jump, but not all of them want to. Some horses rely on their riders to tell them when to take off, others prefer to figure it out for themselves. Luckily, not many horses jump over their fences, even though they successfully clear greater heights out hunting or in the show ring.

When you first learn to jump you may find it easier to use a neck strap to hold onto. You can hold this through all five phases of the jump—approach, take-off, moment of suspension, landing, and the getaway.

Approach

1

Takeoff

2

Moment of suspension

3

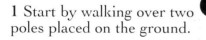

1 Start by walking over two poles placed on the ground.

BUILDING UP

Once your horse will trot over poles on the ground, introduce some wings at each end of both poles. Then turn them into jumps, first by raising the second pole and then by raising both. Always approach jumps calmly and at an even gait. Do not introduce the second jump until your horse is moving smoothly and happily over the first.

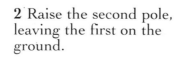

2 Raise the second pole, leaving the first on the ground.

I love jumping, even though I haven't done much of it yet —I think I will try out for the Olympics when I'm older!

3 Raise both poles to form a combination fence.

1 Your position should be balanced, with your legs resting against the horse's sides and your hands in contact with the horse's mouth.

2 At takeoff, fold your body forward so that you take your weight off the horse's loins and are less likely to get "left behind."

POOR SEAT

Try not to stand up in the stirrups or to lean too far back. Concentrate on sitting centrally in the saddle, and use the neck strap to hold onto if you feel unsafe. It won't be long before your movements will automatically follow the horse's.

3 As the horse rounds its back, you should flatten yours, still leaning forward and still with your legs resting against the horse's sides. Keep looking in the direction you are going.

Landing

4

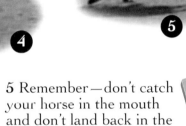

5

Getaway, or recovery

4 As the horse lands, allow it as much rein as it needs. Your body should become more upright. Once it has landed, take up the rein.

5 Remember—don't catch your horse in the mouth and don't land back in the saddle with a thump as you ride your horse forward.

Q Why does my horse sometimes stop or run around the jump?

A There are many reasons why horses fail to jump, but most of them are the fault of the rider. Don't jump the same jump over and over again as this will make your horse fed up. The only way it can tell you it's had enough is to refuse. It could be that you are asking your horse to jump something that is too big for it. You may have accidentally hurt your horse's mouth or landed heavily in the saddle, and it doesn't want it to happen again. Or it may be that you need to be more firm with your aids on the approach to the jump.

Saturday evening
Our trotting poles were being moved too easily in our lesson today, but Marty had a good idea. She made little piles of earth and rested the ends of each pole on the mounds, pushing them down quite firmly. Even when Oscar kicked one of the poles, it didn't move!

23

Hacking

One of the most enjoyable things about riding is going out for a hack. If you are lucky enough to live near countryside—open fields or forests—you probably have many rides to choose from. Hacking is also an excellent way of keeping your horse fit.

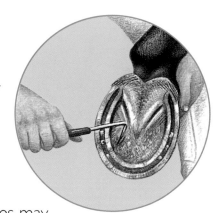

DIFFICULT GROUND

You should always carry a hoof pick in your pocket to remove stones and mud from your horse's hooves. Be careful on muddy ground as mud can be very deep and your horse's shoes may be sucked off. Also, beware of overhanging trees.

Q When hacking I've been told to follow the country code. What is the country code?

A The country code is the way that everyone using the countryside should try and behave.
You can't go wrong if you follow these simple guidelines:

- Always leave gates as you find them.
- Stick to bridle paths if you can.
- Do not ride across growing crops.
- Do not enter a field unless you know it is all right to do so.
- Avoid using very muddy tracks in wet weather.
- Be courteous to others at all times.
- Always slow down when meeting other riders or other users of the countryside.

MEETING PEDESTRIANS

You are likely to meet other people enjoying the countryside when hacking. Make sure you don't gallop past them as you could splash them with mud and frighten them. Always pass people at a walk, and treat them with the same respect that you would want them to show you.

❶

❷

❸

OPENING AND CLOSING A GATE

At some stage on your ride, you will probably have to pass through a gate. It saves time and trouble if you can train your horse to stand still while you unfasten the gate, back away while you open it, and go through quickly before the gate swings back. Make sure you close it properly behind you.

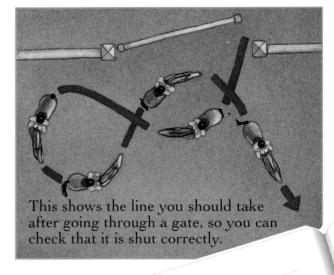

This shows the line you should take after going through a gate, so you can check that it is shut correctly.

UP AND DOWN HILLS

Riding up and down hills is ideal for getting your horse fit. Your position in the saddle is the same whether you are going uphill or down. Your shoulders should always be in front of your hips. Do not lean back in the saddle when going downhill as this puts unnecessary strain on your horse's hindquarters.

Always Remember:

Walk for the last 10-15 minutes of any ride (about half a mile). This is particularly important if the ride has been a fast one and your horse is hot and sweaty. Horses need time to cool off gradually. Unless your horse is really tired, there is no need to get off and lead it, but if you do get off, you should run up the stirrups and loosen the girth.

Thursday
Oscar got a stone in his foot out riding today. I'd forgotten to bring a hoof pick with me and I couldn't get the stone out. It made him quite lame, so we got back really late. I got into real trouble, not because Oscar was lame, but because I had gone for a ride on my own without telling anyone where I was going.
Oops!

Riding on the road

From time to time, most riders have to take their horse or pony on the road. This can be very dangerous. Some motorists don't know how to deal with riders on the road, so all you can do is follow a few simple rules. Make sure you are doing everything you can to keep yourself and your horse safe.

TURNING

Turning right is the easiest maneuver you will have to make when riding on the road. You must follow normal traffic rules and ride on the right. To signal that you are going to make a right turn, simply put both reins in your left hand and extend your right arm outward. Always put your hand back on the rein before making the turn. Whenever you are on the road, you should obey traffic signals and road signs.

Q What else should I remember when I'm out on the road?

A • Ride single file on busy roads.
• On roads that are wide, straight, and quiet, you may ride two abreast.
• It is usually safest to stick to a walk on busy roads, but if you do have to trot, do not go faster than a working trot, and only do so in short bursts.
• Beware of slippery road surfaces.
• Keep to the right-hand side, even when you want to turn left. You can give a left-hand signal while riding on the right. Wait until you are level with the right-hand side of the crossroad before crossing the road. NEVER move into the middle of the road when waiting to turn.

Tuesday
Oscar is so good on the roads and doesn't mind even the largest and noisiest truck. So I was really surprised this morning when he suddenly jumped at something in the hedge and leapt into the road. Luckily, nothing was coming!

COURTESY ON THE ROAD

As a rider, you should keep to the right side of the road, move in single file along busy roads, and give clear signals at all times. Remember to thank other road users for their consideration. You must not ride on footpaths, sidewalks, or trimmed grass shoulders. You can ride on rough shoulders, but be careful of hidden ditches or drains.

HAND SIGNALS

All hand signals should be clear and held long enough to be seen and understood. Use the left and right arms to show in which direction you will be turning.

To slow traffic down, extend your arm and keep it rigid from shoulder to finger tips. Move your arm up and down several times.

To stop traffic, bend your arm and hold the palm of your hand toward the traffic. To stop traffic behind you, turn around in the saddle and use the same signal.

LEADING ON THE ROAD

If you have to lead your horse on the road, always place yourself between it and the traffic. You must still be on the right-hand side of the road, so you are leading your horse from the near, or left-hand, side. Make sure you can both be seen by wearing light-colored or fluorescent clothing.

Sunday
Annabel and I are taking a riding and road safety test. The instructor uses white tape to lay out an imaginary road and asks her friends to pretend to be hazards. It was interesting to see how the ponies reacted. Oscar was terrific as usual.

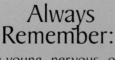

Always Remember:

Put a young, nervous, or inexperienced horse or rider in the middle of a group of riders when riding along a road. Having an experienced rider at the front keeps the pace steady. The rider at the back ensures that no one gets left behind. Stay in single file and do not crowd one another.

CHAPTER 2
Horse care

Owning a horse is something most riders dream about. It is a big responsibility as horses need a lot of care and attention. There are many things to consider before you choose a horse.

Arabian horse

BUY OR LEASE?

Getting a horse on lease means you don't have to begin spending a large amount of money. But its care is your responsibility just as much as if you had bought it. Do not forget that you will have to give the horse back one day.

English pony

WHICH HORSE?

A calm horse is best if you're a nervous rider. If you are experienced, you may want a horse that is more forward going. If the horse will be living in a field all year, a hardy breed would be a good choice. Don't buy a horse that you will quickly grow out of, or a big horse that you plan to "grow into."

13hh chestnut gelding. 9yrs. Excels XC 100% traffic, shoe, etc. $3,000

UNDERSTANDING THE ADS

This ad tells you that the pony is a 9-year-old chestnut gelding (male), 13 hands high. He is good at cross-country, is safe on the road, and is easy to shoe. But there is a lot it doesn't say. For example, is he easy to catch? Make a list of questions to ask the seller.

Q If I find a suitable horse, should I have it examined by a vet?

A It is usually best to get a horse examined. There are different levels of veterinary examinations. Expensive ones are detailed and include X rays. Cheaper ones simply tell you if the horse is fit enough for what you want it to do. Vetting can reveal a problem that means that the horse is not suitable to buy.

Q Should I get my horse insured?

A Yes, you should make sure that you are covered for any damage that your horse may cause to someone else. You can also insure your horse against injury, as vet's fees can be expensive, and for the loss of and damage to your tack.

ACTION

The way a horse moves makes a difference to its fitness, the way it handles, and how comfortable it is to ride. Ask an experienced person to look at the horse's action for you.

✔ GOOD CONFORMATION

Conformation means the way a horse is put together. The horse should look in good proportion and be alert. Its eyes should be large and set well apart. Its feet should point straight ahead and its quarters should be muscular and strong.

✗ Goose rump
Steeply sloping rump from the highest point of the quarters to the tail.

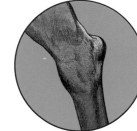

✗ Narrow chest
Its chest should be wide enough to give its heart plenty of room. But a very wide chest can cause it to be an uncomfortable ride.

✗ Capped hocks
Capped hocks look as though they are a serious fault, but they don't actually cause a problem for the horse.

✗ Splints
A splint is a bony swelling on the leg, usually below the knee. Once a splint has formed it is not a serious condition.

quarters

fetlock

✗ Windgalls
A windgall is a soft swelling just above the fetlock. This should not stop you from buying the horse as it is not a serious condition.

✗ Cracked hooves
A horse with brittle hooves might become lame and be difficult to shoe. Strong hooves often mean a healthy horse.

Always Remember:

Take a knowledgeable person with you when you go to look at a horse. Before you go, write down any questions that you need to ask. It is easy to forget questions when you get there. Try not to fall in love with the first horse you see— it is important to keep an open mind. It is a good idea to ask if you can have the horse for two weeks on a trial basis.

Saturday
We went to look at a pony today. She sounded lovely in the ad. The only thing was, she turned out to be just 9 hands high. As one hand is about 4 inches, she was really much too small for me!

Wednesday
Guess what! Mom has ended up buying me Oscar—he's my favorite pony at the riding stable. I still can't believe it. We are boarding him at the riding stable as we don't have a stall or field of our own. It means getting up really early so that I can do his stall before school, but it's worth it.

The stall

A stall is useful but not absolutely necessary in the care of a pony. It is more important in the care of a horse, and should be warm, light, and well drained.

STALL FITTINGS

The stall should be on level ground and have a split door so that your horse can look out. The roof should overhang the front of the stall to protect your horse from the weather. Windows should have bars over them and the floor should be made of concrete, with a built-in drain. Any lights must be out of reach of your horse.

lighting

muck heap

ventilation

manger

haynet

tying ring

water bucket

barred window

kickboard

fresh bedding

split door

tying ring

LAYING BEDS AND MUCKING OUT

1 Every day, take all the droppings and wet bedding out of the stall using a fork and a manure bucket or a wheelbarrow. If you have time, sweep all the bedding to one side to allow the floor to dry.

2 Replace the wet bedding with fresh bedding. When you lay a bed in an empty stall, use as much bedding as you can. Spread it over the floor to make a thick, soft layer. Make banks of bedding around the edges of the stall. Your horse needs less straw in the day than at night.

rake

manure fork

manure bucket

wheelbarrow

broom

shovel

Q What is the best bedding to use?

A Wood shavings are the most common bedding, but you must make sure there are no sharp splinters in it. Sawdust can be used with wood shavings, but it is dusty and can clog up drains. Straw is also generally used for bedding. Shredded paper is popular because it is warm and dust free. But it is also heavy when damp, and some horses may be allergic to the ink in the paper.

Wood shavings

Straw

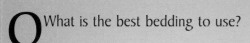

Friday
I'm learning to give Oscar a really comfortable bed. At first, I didn't use enough bedding. Gerry, the owner of the riding stable, had to show me how much to use. She made me build really thick banks around the edges. I had to pat them with the back of my shovel to make them square.

Keeping a horse outdoors

Horses are grazing animals. If possible, fresh grass should always be part of their diet. In moderate climates, horses are healthier if they live outdoors even in winter. Even in harsher climates, horses may spend part of many days out in the field.

TYPES OF GRASS

Old, well-established pastureland is the best grazing for horses. Lots of different grasses will have grown over the years. New grass or grass that has been fertilized could be too rich for your horse.

Horsetail
This weed is most often found on waste ground. It can grow in fields where the grass hasn't been properly cared for.

POISONOUS PLANTS

Some plants are poisonous to horses. Check that there is nothing dangerous growing in or near your field. Ask an adult to help you pull up any dangerous plants and burn them on a bonfire.

White snakeroot
This plant grows on the edge of woodlands. It can be removed by using a herbicide (chemical).

Ragwort
This weed grows on vacant land and in fields. It should be pulled up by the roots and burned.

Deadly nightshade
This plant grows mainly in wooded areas, but should be pulled up if it grows in or near your horse's field.

Red maple
These trees should be fenced off from your horse's field.

CARE OF THE PASTURE

Horses and ponies waste a lot of grass in their field. They often trample good grass and turn other areas sour with their droppings.
Pick up droppings every day using a shovel and a wheelbarrow.
Or you could use heavy waterproof gloves to pick up the droppings.
It is a job well worth doing as it helps to keep the grass and your horse healthy.

RESTING FIELDS

If your riding stable has a lot of grazing land, it may be divided up into smaller fields. Fields that are empty for a while can be sprayed with pesticide (chemical) to get rid of parasites and weeds. Sheep or cattle can be kept in fields with horses. This improves the quality of the grazing since sheep and cattle eat grass that horses leave.

Bracken
This is found on vacant land and in woodland. Bracken is dangerous over a long period of time as it can damage your horse's liver.

Yew
Yew trees are extremely poisonous. If your horse's field borders land where yew trees grow, it is very important to fence them off. Every part of the tree is poisonous—even the twigs.

Black locust
This is found mainly by the side of the road. Your horse must not be allowed to eat it.

1 pm—Oscar was right at the far side of the field this morning. I had to trek through the mud to get him. Next week, he's going into one of the smaller paddocks so that the big field can be rested and given some fertilizer. He'll be with Annabel's pony, Daniel, so he won't get lonely.

Q Is it all right to keep my horse in a field by itself?

A Most horses do not like to be kept on their own. They are herd animals and need company. If there aren't any other horses to share your horse's field, you could put a few sheep, cows, or even a goat in the field.

Sunday
There was a dead bird in Oscar's water trough this morning. Ugh! I got it out and Annabel and I decided that the water might not be very good for the ponies to drink. So we had to empty the trough and clean it out. Now Oscar and Daniel have nice, clean water to drink.

Fencing

The fence around your field must be strong and well built. Inspect it regularly to check for any damage. It does not have to be very high, because even horses that are good at jumping rarely try to jump out. The gate also needs to be strong and easy for you—but not for your horse—to open and close.

TYPES OF FENCING

The best type of fence to use is a strongly built, wooden post-and-rail fence. Fences with three rails are the most popular. Another popular type of fence has plain wire or plastic in place of the wooden rails. Try to avoid barbed wire and wire netting because these can be dangerous for your horse.

✔ Post and rail
This is a safe and secure type of fence. Three rails are better than two.

✔ Post and plastic rail
Broad plastic strips are a cheaper alternative to wooden rails. Plastic strips are better than plain wire fencing because they are seen more easily.

✔ Rail and wire
The wire used in this type of fence must be plain, not barbed. It must also be pulled taut or your horse could get tangled in it.

Q What sort of gate is best for my horse's field?

A The best gate is a five-barred one, which swings open without touching the ground. It should have a latch that your horse cannot open. You can avoid damage to the gate by not climbing over it or sitting on it. If you must climb over it, always do so at the hinge end. Your gate must be wide enough for your horse to pass through easily.

FIELD SECURITY

You must make sure that the gate to your field is always securely shut. Some horses learn how to open gates, so you should fit a horse-proof latch. You could put on a padlock as a precaution against horse thieves. As a further guard, you could get your horse freeze-marked. This involves having your horse permanently marked with a number, usually on its back. If it is stolen and offered for sale, the number makes it easier for the police to know that the horse is yours.

FIELD SHELTER

Most horses don't mind bad weather as long as they have somewhere to shelter from the wind. The side of a building, a high hedge, or a hollow in the ground all offer shelter. A special run-in shelter can provide protection from wind and rain. In summer, your horse can use it to escape from flies and the hot sun.

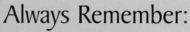

prevailing wind

bedding

Always Remember:

Make sure that your horse has enough to drink. If you are lucky, water will be piped to a trough. These troughs are usually controlled by a valve so that they cannot overflow. Otherwise, you will have to fill your trough regularly using a hose. An old bathtub can be used as a water trough. Make sure that all the faucets have been taken off and that there are no sharp edges for your horse to injure itself on. In the winter you must break the ice in the trough every day.

Morning
I think the stable where Oscar lives is the best in the world. The horses there always look warm and cozy. I spend all the time I can at the stable—Mom says I should take my pajamas with me, because I never want to go home.

Dual system

When you have both a stall and a field, you can give your horse the best of both worlds—living in and living out. This dual system is used by many riding stables and works very well.

Winter

Always Remember :
Lay a good, thick bed, especially on winter nights. A thick bed gives your horse a comfortable resting place if it wants to lie down. Some horses are very restless and paw at their bedding and create bare patches. All you can do is add as much bedding as you can. The daytime bed in summer does not need to be as thick as a nighttime or winter bed. Your horse is less likely to lie down during the day.

HALF IN, HALF OUT
Using the dual system means that your horse spends half the time indoors and half in the field. In the summer, it is best to keep your horse in the stall during the day and out in the field at night. In the winter, your horse is better off in the stall at night. It can go out in the field for exercise during daylight hours.

FULL LIVERY

Full livery is when you hand the daily care of your horse over to the riding stable. The owner of the stable makes sure that it is fed, has new shoes, and is wormed. Everything is done for you. It is not the most popular type of livery as you miss out on all the fun of caring for your horse.

PARTIAL LIVERY

With partial livery, you agree with the owner of the yard exactly how much time you can spend looking after your horse. The staff at the riding stable will do the rest. This could mean that you exercise and muck out every day, but the staff arranges shoeing, worming, and giving feeds at night.

ROUGH BOARD

The cost of rough board covers a stall and grazing for your horse. It should also include space in a hay store for your hay and space in the feed room for your horse's feed. Everything else is your responsibility.

Summer

TACK SECURITY

Tack security is very important. Tack thefts are common, and often the stolen property is not recovered. All your tack should be marked with your name and other identifying marks in permanent pen. Any other belongings that you leave at the stables—rugs, bandages, etc.—should carry identification. If you can, store your tack in a locked room. In some stables, security lights and guard dogs discourage thieves.

Later
The tack room at our stable is a sort of double room. The inside is like a big walk-in closet. It has a lock, and everyone keeps saddles and bridles in there. We have bridle hooks and saddle racks with our horses' names on them. In the outer room we keep things like rugs, hats, and grooming kits.

Grooming

Most horses enjoy being groomed—some even fall asleep while you work. Grooming keeps the skin healthy and the coat shiny. Daily grooming ensures that you notice any cuts or other problems as early as possible.

Stable rubber

Sponges

Dandy brush

Hoof oil and brush

Hoof pick

Body brush

Water brush

Curry comb (metal)

Sweat scraper

Curry comb (rubber)

Mane comb

Mane-pulling comb

QUICK-RELEASE KNOT

When tying a horse up, always use a quick-release knot, as shown on the left. It will hold your horse securely. To undo the knot, remove the loose end from the loop and tug it sharply. A quick-release knot like this may be necessary if your horse gets tangled up in any way.

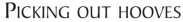

PICKING OUT HOOVES

Cleaning out your horse's hooves is something you should never forget to do. Work from the back of the foot toward the toe using a metal hoof pick. Pay special attention to the grooves on each side of the center "V" of the foot, called the frog.

Grooming kit
To make sure you don't lose any items in your grooming kit, keep them all together in a grooming box. If your horse is at a livery stable, write your name or your horse's name on each piece of equipment.

Always Remember:

Attach a loop of baler twine to each metal tie ring in your stall. Tie your horse to the twine, not to the metal ring. If your horse is frightened and pulls back suddenly, the twine will break and your horse will not injure itself. Your haynet should also be tied to a baler twine loop.

ORDER OF GROOMING

The usual order of grooming is to work from the top of the head to the hindquarters. Do this first on one side and then on the other. Use the body brush to brush the head, mane, and tail. Finish off the body with the stable rubber. Sponge the eyes, nose, and dock area (under the tail).

6.30 pm—I think Oscar must look for the muddiest part of the field before getting down to roll. I always seem to work harder than anyone else at getting him clean. I am just thankful that he isn't a gray. Getting rid of grass stains takes forever!

PULLING THE MANE

You only need to pull your horse's mane if it is very thick or tangled. The purpose is to shorten it, make it lie flat, or make it easier to braid. Wrap a few hairs at a time around a comb and pull them out. Only pull the long hairs from underneath.

Q Is grooming a grass-kept horse any different from grooming a stabled horse?

A With a grass-kept horse, you can use a dandy brush directly on the coat. If your horse is very muddy, you can use a plastic or rubber curry comb on it. Take care not to groom a grass-kept horse too vigorously as it needs the natural grease in its coat to keep it warm and dry. Never pull a grass-kept horse's tail as it needs a full tail for protection from flies and the weather.

OILING HOOVES

Your horse will look very sharp when its hooves are oiled. This is nearly always done before a show. Be careful not to oil the hooves too often. Spreading a thin film of oil over them stops them from absorbing water. This can make them brittle.

Use a dandy brush to remove mud from a grass-kept horse.

Use a body brush or an old, soft dandy brush on the tail—never use a mane comb.

Use separate, differently colored sponges for the head and dock areas.

Pick out your horse's feet every day.

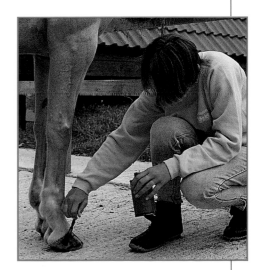

Tack

There are so many different items of tack that you may find it difficult to know what is best for your horse. Always ask for help from someone who really understands what each item is used for. It is very important to look after your tack properly.

Q How often should I clean my tack?

A If you want to be a perfectionist, the answer is every time you use it. This may be unrealistic, but you should aim to clean it once a week. It helps if you can rinse the bit and wipe mud from the tack after every ride. Inspect your saddle and bridle for damage each time you clean them.

TYPES OF GIRTH

The most popular girth is made of synthetic fabric and has a soft, strong filling. Other girths are made from leather, webbing, or string. Leather girths need a lot of care to keep them supple. String girths can pinch your horse.

STIRRUP IRONS

Stirrup irons should be made from stainless steel. They must be large enough to leave about ¹/2 in (1 cm) clear on either side of your boot at its widest part. If they are bigger, your whole foot could slip through. If they are smaller, your foot could get stuck.

Plain iron

Simplex safety iron

Safety iron

Always Remember:

Make sure that the hairs on your horse's back lie the right way under the saddle. To do this, place the saddle well up on the withers and push it back into place. If you use a saddle cloth, it should be slightly bigger than the saddle, and must not press on the horse's backbone.

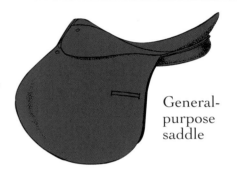

General-purpose saddle

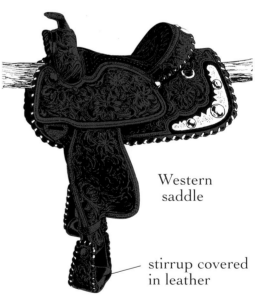

Western saddle

stirrup covered in leather

withers

saddle cloth

TYPES OF SADDLE

General-purpose saddles are the most widely used. These are usually made of leather and are shaped to encourage the rider to sit in a balanced position. Western saddles are very comfortable for both the rider and the horse.

PUTTING ON THE BRIDLE

The main purpose of the bridle is to hold the bit in the correct position in your horse's mouth. The browband holds the headpiece in place behind your horse's ears. The cheekpieces can be adjusted to raise or lower the bit in the mouth. The throatlatch, which is part of the headpiece, prevents the bridle from coming off. The reins link the rider to the bit. Always loop the reins over your horse's neck when you put the bridle on.

Hold the headpiece with your right hand. Lift it to the level of your horse's ears. Give the bit to your horse with your left hand.

As soon as the bit is in your horse's mouth, put the headpiece over its ears.

Do up the throatlatch. There should be room for one hand's width between it and your horse's jawbone.

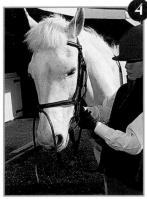

Do up the noseband. You should be able to insert two fingers between it and your horse's face.

Pelham bridle

NOSEBANDS

A simple noseband (or cavesson) is just for show as it is not needed to keep the bridle on. A drop noseband is used to stop a horse from opening its mouth so wide that the bit has no effect. Grakle nosebands work in the same way as a drop noseband. They have two nosebands, which cross over at the front.

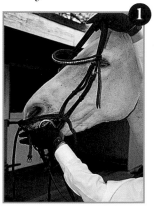

Drop noseband

Grakle noseband

TYPES OF BIT

The most common bit is the jointed snaffle. It presses on the corners of the mouth and the tongue. A curb bit has a curb chain. Pressure on the reins causes the curb chain to tighten in the chin groove to make your horse bring its nose in. A Pelham bit combines the actions of a curb bit and a snaffle bit.

Jointed snaffle bit

Pelham bit

curb chain

Curb bit

Mom bought me some second-hand stirrup leathers. They've been looked after so well that they're lovely and soft!

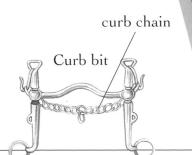

41

Feeding

In the wild, horses and ponies find their food wherever they can. They cover large areas of land as they search for food. The food they find is quite varied—from sweet meadow grasses to the leaves and bark of trees. The variety gives them all the vitamins and minerals they need to stay healthy. Your horse, however, relies on you to control its diet.

Q What is hard food?

A Hard food is another name for concentrated food. Oats are the best all-around food but may be too rich for some horses. Barley is less rich than oats and is very useful for horses that lose weight easily. Cubes (pellets) or mixed food can be given instead of the actual grain. In both cases, the manufacturer uses different grains and a careful balance of vitamins and minerals in the feed. Ask an experienced person to help you choose the right feed for your horse.

Chaff and molasses meal

Corn

Bran

Barley

Dried alfalfa

Grass

Hay

BULK FEED

The basis of a horse's diet is bulk food, such as grass and hay. The choice of any additional food you give your horse depends on the work it does and the type of horse it is. A very active horse needs a diet made up of 60% bulk food and 40% hard food. A horse that is out in a field as a break from normal work needs a diet of just bulk food. Ask an experienced person what the balance should be for your horse.

Winter feeding

	8 a.m.	Noon	4 p.m.	8 p.m.
14 hh pony 825 lb (375 kg) Stabled, hacking, some jumping. **FEED 19.5 lb (9 kg) per day**	2 lb (1 kg) hard food 4.5 lb (2 kg) hay	No hard food 2 lb (1 kg) hay	4.5 lb (2 kg) hard food No hay	No hard food 6.5 lb (3 kg) hay
12 hh pony 660 lb (300 kg) In at night, out during the day. Light hacking. **FEED 16 lb (7.4 kg) per day**	No hard food 4.5 lb (2 kg) hay in field	No hard food No hay	2 lb (1 kg) hard food 2 lb (1 kg) hay	No hard food 7.5 lb (3.4 kg) hay

Summer feeding

	8 a.m.	Noon	4 p.m.	8 p.m.
14 hh pony 825 lb (375 kg) Stabled daytime, out at night. Hacking, shows. **FEED 19.5 lb (9 kg) per day**	4.5 lb (2 kg) hard food 6.5 lb (3 kg) hay	No hard food No hay	2 lb (1 kg) hard food No hay	Turn out to pasture; grass is remainder of ration
12 hh pony 660 lb (300 kg) Out all the time. Light work, some shows. **FEED 16 lb (7.4 kg) per day**	2 lb (1 kg) hard food No hay	Grass makes up rest of daily ration	Grass makes up rest of daily ration	Grass makes up rest of daily ration

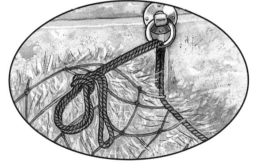

HAY

The customary hay for horses is meadow hay. Alfalfa (lucerne) is similar to hay. It contains lots of calcium, so horses fed on alfalfa need a smaller amount of hard food. You should feed hay in a haynet that is tied with a quick-release knot.

FEED QUANTITY

The chart above gives you an idea of what to feed two ponies of different heights and living arrangements. No two horses are the same. Some put on weight much more easily than others. Whatever your feeding routine, you must always provide fresh water for your horse.

I still can't believe how much water Oscar can drink— especially when we come back from a fast ride!

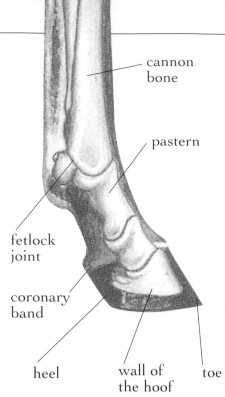

cannon bone

pastern

fetlock joint

coronary band

heel

wall of the hoof

toe

Feet and shoes

There is a saying, "No foot, no horse," and this is very true. A horse's feet need special care if it is to be healthy and capable of work. Hooves grow all the time, like fingernails. A good farrier will make sure that your horse has healthy feet and shoes that fit properly. Shoes stop your horse's feet from wearing down too fast when it is ridden on hard surfaces.

THE FOOT

Underneath your horse's foot you will see a soft V-shape, which extends from the heel toward the toe. This is the frog. It absorbs shock and improves the circulation of blood in the foot. The bars and the wall of the hoof give the foot strength. Your horse has no feeling in this part of its hoof, so it does not hurt your horse to have nails put in to keep the shoes on.

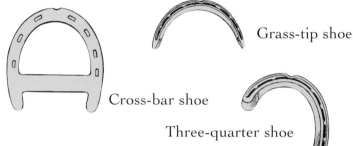

Grass-tip shoe

Cross-bar shoe

Three-quarter shoe

TYPES OF SHOE

Horseshoes are made of iron and have a groove in them to stop the horse from slipping. Cross-bar shoes and three-quarter shoes are used on horses with damaged feet. Grass-tip shoes are used on horses living out and not being ridden, to give protection to the front part of the foot.

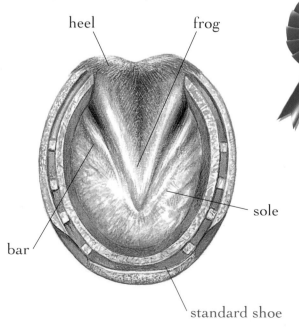

heel

frog

sole

bar

standard shoe

Always Remember:

Check and clean out your horse's feet every day. You need a hoof pick to remove mud and stones that get packed into the hollows between the frog and the wall. Use the hoof pick from the heel to the toe of each foot in turn. Sweep up the pickings afterward. You can paint the outside of the hoof with hoof oil to make your horse's feet look sharp. It is a good idea to carry a hoof pick in your pocket when out riding. You never know when you might need it.

FOOT PROBLEMS

Some foot problems can be remedied by changing your horse's diet. Others need the attention of a good farrier. Sand cracks are cracks that run down from the top of the hoof. They are a serious condition. Grass cracks run upward from the ground and are less serious. If you are unsure of what to do about a foot problem, ask your farrier for advice.

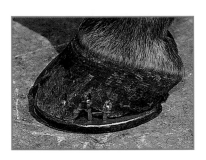

Q How often should the farrier tend my horse?

A You will need to call the farrier every four to eight weeks. Check your horse's shoes daily. If the hoof wall sticks out over the shoe, the foot needs trimming. Other signs that your horse needs new shoes include: the shoes clicking, your horse stumbling a lot, clenches (risen nails) sticking up from the wall of the hoof, thin shoes, and loose shoes.

healthy foot

grass cracks

TYPES OF STUD

There are two types of stud—the road stud and the competition stud. Both give your horse extra grip. Studs are only used in the hind shoes. Road studs are shallow with a hard tip. Competition studs are pointed, for use in hard, dry conditions, or large and square, for use in mud.

Road stud

Competition stud

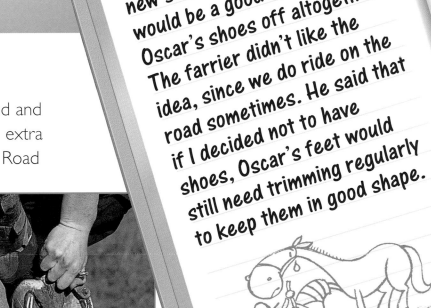

7 pm—Today Oscar has a new set of shoes. I asked if it would be a good idea to leave Oscar's shoes off altogether. The farrier didn't like the idea, since we do ride on the road sometimes. He said that if I decided not to have shoes, Oscar's feet would still need trimming regularly to keep them in good shape.

Health check

Your horse cannot tell you if it is feeling ill. It is up to you to recognize signs of sickness and be ready to obtain a treatment or call a vet. Luckily, most horses and ponies remain healthy and are usually fit and active well into old age.

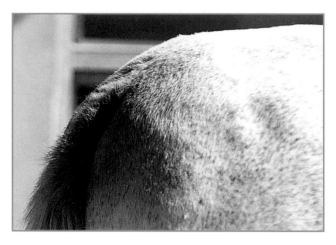

HEAD CHECK

A healthy horse's eyes are wide open and bright. Its ears should be pricked and it should be alert. The nostrils should be free from discharge. Breathing should be quiet and even. A sick horse will seem listless and dull eyed. It will show little interest in its surroundings. There could be discharge from its eyes or nose.

COAT CHECK

A healthy horse has a sleek, flat coat and supple skin. Horses can get a condition called sweet itch (above). They get so itchy that they can rub all the hair from their tail or mane. If your horse's coat is dull and it seems to be sweating, then there may be something wrong. If there is no experienced person around to advise you, always call the vet.

3 pm—Oscar seemed a bit lame today. When we looked him over, we couldn't find anything wrong. His legs weren't hot or swollen, and he hadn't gotten a stone in his shoe. He must have stepped on something sharp. We're going to give him a rest tomorrow and see how he is the next day.

Always Remember:

Check for saddle or girth galls if your horse is overweight or has not been ridden for a while. These are small, painful swellings on the skin that form under the saddle and girth. This mainly happens in the spring, when horses eat lots of new grass and put on weight. The condition is made worse by badly-fitting or dirty tack. If the skin is broken, bathe it gently in a mild antiseptic solution. Do not use the saddle on the horse until the sores have completely healed.

Q Do I need to vaccinate my horse?

A Yes. Vaccination will protect your horse against equine flu and an illness called tetanus. It also may not be able to go to some shows and competitions without a valid vaccination certificate.

GENERAL HEALTH

Horses are generally healthy and are rarely ill. If a horse is limping, the cause is most likely to be in the foot, but you should check the lower legs for heat or swelling. You can apply a poultice to reduce swelling, but lameness usually is treated by rest.

Later
Oscar had his flu shot today. It was really amazing. The vet just patted him on the neck, talking to him all the time, and the next thing I knew he was screwing a syringe into the needle that was sticking into Oscar's neck. I don't think Oscar felt a thing.

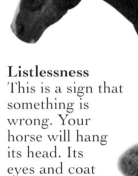

Listlessness
This is a sign that something is wrong. Your horse will hang its head. Its eyes and coat will look dull. It will have no interest in what is going on.

Lameness
Check that nothing is stuck in the foot. Rest is the best cure for lameness.

Off feed
This could mean your horse has an internal problem. Drinking much more water than normal can also mean that something is wrong.

TEETH CHECK

Your horse's teeth continue to grow throughout its life. The front teeth are used to pull grass or hay. The back teeth grind the food before it is swallowed. Sometimes, the teeth develop sharp edges. Occasionally a back tooth will grow so long that it damages the tongue and the inside of the cheek. Your horse should have a regular visit from the horse dentist so that its teeth can be rasped (have sharp edges removed).

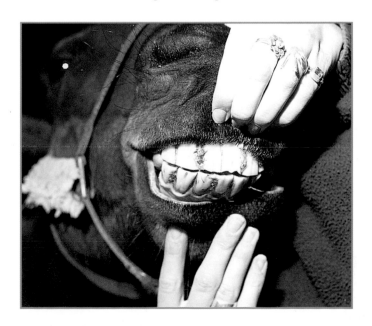

Protective clothing

We expect our horses to do things they would never do in the wild. We clip their coats and take them traveling, pull their manes and tails, and teach them to jump. It is only fair that you protect your horse from injury by providing it with rugs, bandages, and other forms of clothing.

Thursday
I asked Gerry, who owns the stable, whether Oscar should have a New Zealand rug. She said that as he was a hardy English pony, he did not need one. I think she's right because she has other English ponies. None of them wears a blanket and they're all very healthy.

BLANKETS

One popular blanket is the New Zealand rug. It is designed to be warm and waterproof and will not slip even if your horse is galloping in a field. If your horse is stabled, it needs a night blanket and a wool or quilted day banket. These are not waterproof. Antisweat sheets prevent chills and are used on a sweaty horse. In warm weather, a summer sheet provides protection against flies. All blankets must fit properly.

LEG BANDAGES

There are two types of leg bandage—the stable bandage and the exercise bandage. Stable bandages are usually made from wool. They are used with some form of padding to make cold, wet legs warm and dry. It is important not to put the bandage on too tightly— you could damage the leg. Exercise bandages are slightly elasticized and are also used with padding. They support the leg, but should not be left on longer than necessary.

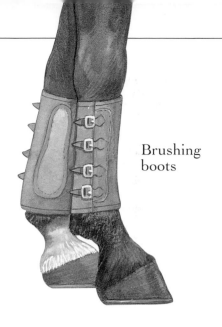

Brushing boots

Overreach boots

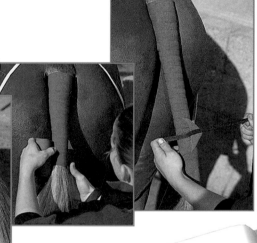

BOOTS

Brushing boots protect the leg from being injured by the opposite leg. They are fastened with leather or velcro straps. Fetlock boots, kneecaps, and hock boots are all designed to protect the joints. Overreach boots are bell-shaped and made of rubber. They cover the hoof and prevent the heels of the front feet from being damaged by the hind hooves.

TAIL BANDAGE

Tail bandages help to keep the top of the tail neat and tidy during travel. Wrap it around the tail from as high up the dock (the area at the top of your horse's tail) as possible. When you get to the end of the tail bone, tie it in place. Don't put it on too tightly or leave it on for any longer than necessary. To remove it, hold it at the top and pull it downward.

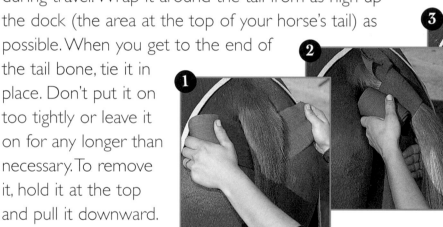

TRAVELING

When traveling in a horse trailer, your horse needs protection from bumps. It should wear a lightweight blanket, even in warm weather. Fit a tail guard over the tail bandage. This attaches to the back of the rug with straps. Traveling boots protect the legs from just above the knee to the top of the hoof. They should be removed as soon as the trip is over. If your horse is likely to throw its head up, you can protect the top of its head with a poll guard. This fastens to the head collar.

Sunday
Gerry took us to a forest for a change of scenery. She loaded the ponies into a horse trailer and off we went. We had a great time. Gerry loaned me some traveling boots for Oscar. They made him walk strangely —it was so funny!

CHAPTER 3
The big event

There is likely to be a time when you think about entering competitions on your horse. Remember, it's not winning but taking part that makes competing so much fun.

FIND OUT WHAT'S ON

Most organizers advertise their events in a local newspaper. Events usually fall into one of three categories—horse shows, hunter trials, or one-day events. Horse shows are a mixture of showing, jumping, and gymkhana games. Hunter trials are a cross-country competition, and one-day events include dressage, show jumping, and cross-country.

WHAT TO ENTER

First you need to get a schedule from the organizers of the classes that are going to be held. Look carefully at the classes to see which ones suit you best. A nice-looking, reliable horse that is a steady jumper may be well-suited to a Working Pony Hunter class. Show jumping is a good choice if your horse is quick, agile, and doesn't knock down fences too often. Most horses enjoy cross-country, which involves jumping solid jumps, ditches, and sometimes water. All-round ponies suit the Best Pony Club Pony class. Little, quick ponies are often good at gymkhana games, especially if you are as active as they are. Make sure you check the timing of the classes (see page 54).

Tuesday
I'm going to enter lots of shows this season. My friend Annabel says that Oscar should do the Working Pony Hunter class because he's such a safe jumper. He hardly ever knocks down any fences.

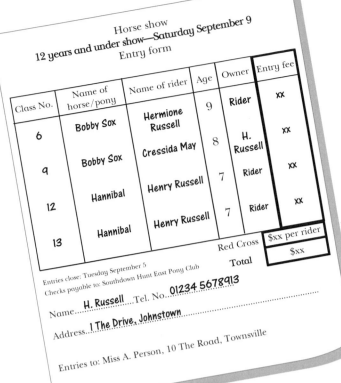

Horse show
12 years and under show—Saturday September 9
Entry form

Class No.	Name of horse/pony	Name of rider	Age	Owner	Entry fee
6	Bobby Sox	Hermione Russell	9	Rider	xx
9	Bobby Sox	Cressida May	8	H. Russell	xx
12	Hannibal	Henry Russell	7	Rider	xx
13	Hannibal	Henry Russell	7	Rider	xx
				Red Cross	$xx per rider
				Total	$xx

Entries close: Tuesday September 5
Checks payable to: Southdown Hunt East Pony Club

Name...H. Russell...Tel. No...01234 5678913

Address..1 The Drive, Johnstown.....

Entries to: Miss A. Person, 10 The Road, Townsville

FILL IN THE FORM

Every schedule should come with an entry form. You must fill in the classes you want to enter, the name of your horse and its rider, the rider's age, and the horse's owner. More than one horse or rider can be entered on the same form. Make sure that the check is completed correctly and return it with the form to the organizer before the closing date.

Always Remember:

Keep your horse interested in what it is doing. Practice makes perfect, but not if you jump the same jump over and over again. Even the happiest horse will get bored and start refusing. Try to think of exciting things for your horse to do. For example, when out hacking, jump fallen logs to add variety to your ride. It is also a good idea to ride through small streams to get your horse used to water.

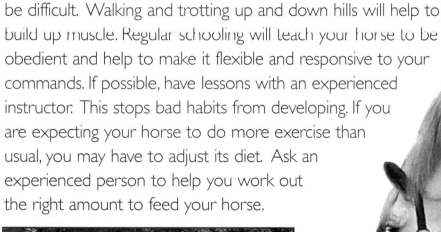

HORSE FITNESS

If your horse is ridden regularly and is on the right diet, getting and keeping it fit should not be difficult. Walking and trotting up and down hills will help to build up muscle. Regular schooling will teach your horse to be obedient and help to make it flexible and responsive to your commands. If possible, have lessons with an experienced instructor. This stops bad habits from developing. If you are expecting your horse to do more exercise than usual, you may have to adjust its diet. Ask an experienced person to help you work out the right amount to feed your horse.

4 pm—I did a really good job braiding Oscar's mane once I got the hang of it. I only had to redo two braids, so I was quite pleased. I did them the night before the show and covered them with some old nylon stockings to keep them tidy.

Getting ready

The secret of having a good time at a show is one word—preparation. If you allow enough time to get both yourself and your horse ready, you will arrive at the show in the right state of mind. Here's how you do it...

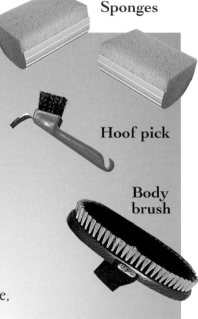

Sponges

Hoof pick

Body brush

Q What grooming kit do I need to take with me?

A You will need a body brush, stable rubber, hoof pick, and hoof oil. You will also need sponges to wipe around your horse's eyes, nostrils, and dock area (under its tail). In a cross-country competition, it helps to have a water carrier and bucket, together with a large sponge, for sponging your horse down.

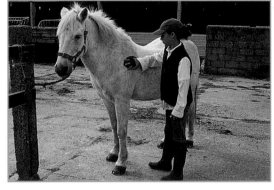

GROOMING

Grooming for a show is not very different from the grooming you give your horse every day. Any light-colored hair on your horse, such as its socks (white markings on its legs), may need special care to remove grass stains. You can use powdered chalk as extra whitening.

Q What other preparations do I need?

A It sounds obvious, but try to get a good night's sleep the night before a show. It is easy to get so excited about the next day that sleep won't come. Go to bed at your normal time, take a warm drink, have a hot bath (anything that makes you relax), set the alarm, and go to sleep. You will have a far better time if you are wide awake and thinking clearly for the competition.

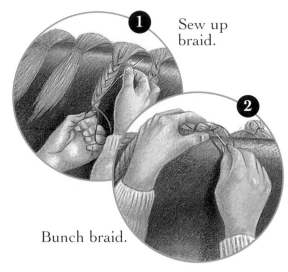

① Sew up braid.

② Bunch braid.

BRAIDING THE MANE AND TAIL

Divide the well-brushed mane into evenly sized bunches. Tightly braid each bunch. Use a needle and thread to sew up the end (step 1, left). Turn the end under, roll it up, and stitch it firmly in place (step 2, left). For the tail, braid it from the top, drawing in hairs evenly from each side (right). Before you reach the end of the tail bone, stop drawing in side hairs and make a thin braid the length of the tail. Tuck it under to form a loop. Stitch in place.

CLEANING TACK

If you are going to clean your tack properly, you must take it apart. So it is important that you learn how to put it together again first. Wash all the metalwork in soapy water. Rinse it well and dry thoroughly. If the leather is muddy,

remove mud with a damp cloth. Rub saddle soap into the leather with a slightly damp sponge. If there is any foam at all, your sponge is too wet. You can put your saddle pads and cloth girth in the washing machine. Leather girths should be saddle-soaped.

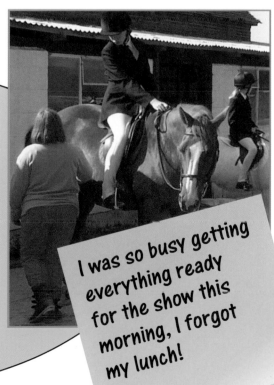

Always Remember:

Get everything ready the night before. You do not want to have to hunt for anything just when you should calmly be eating your breakfast. Clean your jodhpur boots, brush your jacket and hat, and check that you have a clean shirt the night before the show. Have you got two riding gloves or is one still somewhere at the back of the closet, where you tossed it last time you wore it? You will still have to clean your horse, so it may help to pack all your show clothes into a carryall and take them with you to the stable. Then you can change into them once your horse is ready. Don't forget to put some money in your pocket, as well as a clean handkerchief.

I was so busy getting everything ready for the show this morning, I forgot my lunch!

Show day

This is the day you have been waiting for, and you want to enjoy every minute. If you have chosen your events carefully and allowed yourself plenty of time, it should be a memorable and fun occasion.

TIMING

At horse shows there are often many classes taking place at the same time in separate rings. If you enter a lot of classes, you may find that two of them take place at the same time. You won't be able to get your entry money back if you have to miss a class. So take care when choosing which classes to enter. It is best to allow roughly an hour for each class. If you are entering a dressage competition, you will be assigned an exact time. You should present yourself to the dressage steward at least ten minutes beforehand.

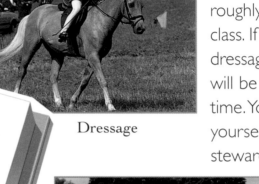
Dressage

Saturday evening
What an amazing day—my first show! I won two 3rds and a 6th, which were three ribbons more than I had hoped for. One of the 3rds was in the Working Pony Hunter class and the other two ribbons were for gymkhana events. Clever, clever Oscar!

Show jumping

Lining up for the judge

Q How do I know when it is my turn to jump in a jumping class?

A The warmup ring is where you can warm up your horse before it is your turn to jump. The warmup ring steward sits at the entrance to the ring. He or she has a blackboard with the numbers of the competitors in the order that they will jump. You have to give your number to the steward. As competitors complete their rounds, the steward crosses off their numbers. Look at the blackboard, see which numbers are before you, and be ready when those competitors enter the ring.

OUTSIDE THE RING

When you get to the horse show, visit the secretary's tent and collect your number. This will be a cardboard number that is worn around your waist. At a cross-country event, your number will be on a bib or tabard, so that it is displayed front and back. You will probably be asked for a deposit for this, which you'll get back when you return your number. When you are not actually taking part in

a class, make sure you don't tire out your horse or disturb other competitors and spectators by riding up and down the field.

Sunday
Before entering the jumping competition I got some practice in the clear-round jumping. I paid an entry fee, did my round, and would have won a clear-round ribbon if Oscar hadn't knocked the last pole down. But it was good practice for the proper jumping competition.

Always Remember:

Smile at the judge if you are awarded a prize and say, "Thank you" when given your ribbon. When everyone has been given their ribbons, you may be asked to do a victory lap. This doesn't mean galloping madly around the arena. Instead, you should follow one another at a controlled canter. The winner usually does another lap alone, while the others leave the arena.

THE PARKING LOT

Your horse trailer should be parked so that there is enough room for your horse to be tied to the outside of it without interfering with the next trailer. If there is a long time between classes, you should give your horse a haynet. Your tack and grooming kit can be stored either inside or under the trailer. Make sure

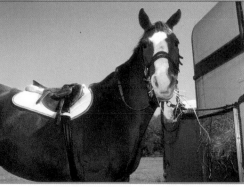

they are somewhere where your horse cannot step on them. It is best if someone can stay near the trailer all the time.

Don't leave your saddle on the ground, where it could get damaged (above). Make sure your horse is happy before chatting with your friends (right).

After the show

Whether you have a good day or a disastrous one, you and your horse will both be feeling very tired. It is important to take good care of your horse while you are still at the show and also once you are back at home.

Evening

We sang songs all the way home from the show. The ponies must have thought we were crazy! I put Oscar in the stable and gave him some water (which he turned up his nose at) before his feed. He really enjoyed his food, and it was dark by the time he finished. I thought I should leave him in tonight, but he was really eager to get into the field. He can have a rest tomorrow.

THE END OF THE DAY

When you have finished your classes, make sure your horse is comfortable. Remove saddle and bridle, and take out studs (see p. 63). An unpicker is useful to take out the braids. If your horse is very hot, cool it down with a sponge wrung out in cold water. Put on a summer sheet or rug. Leave your horse tied to the trailer and give it a haynet. Once you are ready to leave, put on your horse's traveling gear.

1 Sweat scraper
Use this to remove any excess sweat. It is a useful tool to have, but not an essential one.

4 Turn out into the field
Horses that live out should be let into their field after they've been fed and checked over.

2 Wash
After a cross-country round, your horse will be sweating hard and puffing. Use a sponge or an old towel to wipe over its body and legs with cold water.

3 Dry
Use an old towel to get rid of the water before putting on a sweat sheet.

CHECK YOUR HORSE

Back at the stable, unload your horse from the trailer and take off its tail guard and traveling boots. If you haven't already done so, take out the braids and brush out the mane and tail. In the stable, remove the rug and brush your horse with a body brush. Pay special attention to the legs. Pick out the hooves. Put on a night rug and give your horse water and a final feed. Hang up a haynet, then leave your horse in peace.

FINAL FEED

Your horse won't need more than its usual feed after a show. Extra feed can do more harm than good. Horses that live out can be given their feed before being turned out. Offer fresh water first. Your horse will roll when you put it in the field. This is its way of relaxing.

Q What sort of injuries should I look for after the show?

A Your horse is unlikely to damage itself at an ordinary horse show, especially if it has done no more than take part in a showing class, a jumping class, and a few gymkhana events. At a cross-country event, where you will have been jumping fixed fences, it is easy for your horse to knock itself. You should check its legs for any painful areas or cuts. Bad knocks will show up the next morning, so you should examine the legs for swelling and lumps. Treat minor cuts by bathing them gently in salted water. It is unlikely that there will be any serious injuries, but if there is anything you are unsure about, call your veterinarian.

Monday
Dad made me a big bulletin board for my room. At first it only had photos of Oscar on it. But now it has my three ribbons. I've written down details about the show on the back of the ribbons. Now I'll always remember when Oscar and I won them and what we won them for.

Gymkhana events

Gymkhana games are likely to be your first taste of competition. Even if you need to be led on a lead rope, you can still take part. However, most events also require a lot of skill, fitness, and riding ability, as you'll soon find out.

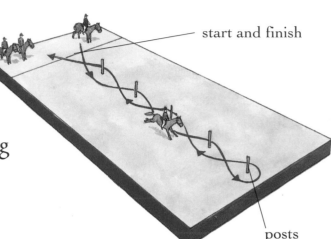

start and finish

posts

PRECISION GAMES

These games can involve balancing a ball on a cone or running along a line of stepping stones (right) without making a mistake. A steady, obedient horse will be more successful than a very fast one. It is best to concentrate on not making a mistake before trying to speed up.

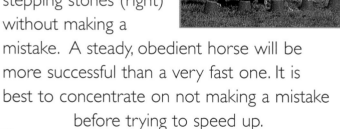

SPEED GAMES

In these games, speed is more important than accuracy. In bending races, for example, each rider has to weave in and out of a line of barrels or posts as quickly as possible. In most races you race against other riders. The races are not timed, so to win you must finish ahead of your rivals.

Lunchtime
Annabel and I are madly practicing gymkhana games. It's more fun when we do it together, and even better when other people join in.

MIXED GAMES

These races combine precision and speed—racing to put a flag into a cone as quickly as possible, for example. All games need practice if you are to have success. You could join a Pony Club games team to improve your technique.

NECK-REINING

When you first start doing gymkhana games, you will find it difficult to control your horse without dropping equipment. You will have to practice neck-reining. Hold the reins in one hand (usually the left) and move that hand across the withers. The pressure on your horse's neck tells it which way to go. Your other hand is then free to hold the equipment.

withers

Q How can I practice without the proper equipment?

A You can easily make or find gymkhana equipment. Buckets, tennis balls, and old socks are easy to find. You can make an old sock bulkier by stuffing the toe with newspaper before rolling it up. For a flag, attach a scrap of cloth to a bamboo pole. Half-fill an old detergent bottle with sand for practicing the bottle race. Cones can be bought quite cheaply from hardware stores. Bean poles make good bending poles. You may be able to buy them at a garden center.

I did it! I did it! I actually managed to vault onto Oscar. The real secret is to keep Oscar moving at a brisk trot.

VAULTING

Some games call for the rider to get off to pick something up before remounting and riding to the finish. Races are often lost by hopping around an excited horse, with one foot in the stirrup, trying to get on. Vaulting is something anyone can do, once the technique has been learned. It's worth spending some time practicing.

Vaulting 2
Swing your right leg over the saddle. Use the hand on the saddle to steady yourself and the horse's forward movement to carry you up.

Vaulting 1
Hold the reins and saddle as shown. Run beside your horse as it trots along. As the near forefoot (front foot nearest to you) hits the ground, push off with both feet and spring up.

Direction of horse

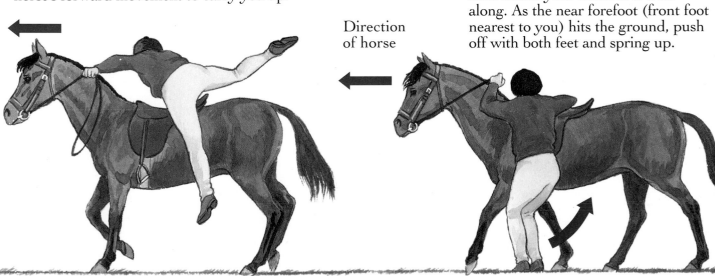

The show ring

A showing class gives you the chance to display your horse and your riding skills. It will also let you see how your horse measures up against others. Here are a few things to remember when in a show ring.

Wednesday
I have decided that showing can be a bit boring. You spend a lot of time standing in a line doing nothing. Even so, Oscar and I entered a Best Pony Club pony showing event at the last show. It was good fun and we came in 7th out of 42 entries. It was only our first time, so I was pretty pleased!

THE SALUTE

Riders sometimes salute to tell the judge they've finished their display. To do a salute, stand squarely in front of the judge. Hold the reins in your right hand and extend your other hand straight down (above right). Bow your head at the same time.

hard hat

beige jodhpurs

tie worn with a white or pastel shirt

jacket, either tweed, black, or navy blue

polished jodhpur boots

BEHAVIOR IN THE SHOW RING

Ride around the ring at the same pace as the other riders. Leave one horse's length between you and the horse in front. Always make sure your horse looks its best; you never know when the judge is looking at you.

Thursday
I picked up lots of schedules at the last show, so Annabel and I are having fun deciding which ones to go to. Next week, there's show jumping at the Old Oaks Equestrian Center. There's even a pairs class, so the show seems just right for us.

PERFORMING A TEST

The judge may ask you to show your horse's paces. To do this, do a circuit of the ring at walk, trot, and canter. Next, canter a figure-eight. Remember to slow down to a trot before you change the rein (direction). Halt by the judge, rein back (walk backward) a few steps, and return to your place.

1 Warming up
You should allow at least half an hour to warm up your horse. This gets the stiffness out of its joints and helps it move easily.

2 The show
This is your chance to let the judge see how well-schooled and obedient your horse is. Try to be calm and confident.

STRIPPING OFF

If the judge wants to see your horse without its saddle, take off the saddle, saddle pad, and martingale (if it wears one). Wait for an assistant to join you in the ring with a body brush and a stable rubber. Brush out the saddle mark. The judge will want to see your horse led away from and toward him or her. Make sure you take the reins over your horse's head to do this. You must also hold your horse steady while the judge examines it.

THE JUDGE

Your attitude toward the judge is something you develop in your first few shows. It's best not to argue with the judge's decision. All show judging is different and a lot depends on whether the judge likes your sort of horse. Always smile and thank the judge before you leave the ring.

Show jumping

This is the most popular form of competitive riding. It is available at many different levels and can be held inside or outside. It is enjoyed equally by novice and experienced riders. Most ponies and horses seem to enjoy it as much as their owners.

THE COURSE

Indoor show jumping usually has tricky, twisty courses in a small arena. Outdoor arenas usually have a free-flowing course with fewer sharp turns. All course designers try to build a course that will produce perhaps ten clear-rounds, a jump-off against the clock, and corners that can be cut.

finish

start

jump-off route

first-round route

WALK THE COURSE

Never be tempted to skip this preparation for show jumping. Once you're in the ring, it's easy to lose your way. Walking the course helps you remember where all the jumps are. It also gives you an idea of any problems you might come across, so that you can decide how to tackle them. In combinations (two jumps placed close together), pace out the distance between the two jumps. Then ask an experienced person to help you work out whether you should kick your horse on at one point, or let it take an extra stride between the two jumps.

Monday
I didn't really understand what unrated jumping was. Then my instructor, Gerry, explained that it was for people like us whose ponies are not registered jumping ponies. In rated jumping, the rules are really strict. I think Oscar and I will stick to unrated.

Q How should I warm up for show jumping?

A As you get to know your horse, you will find out how much warmup it requires. If there is plenty of room at the show, it might be best to take your horse away from the other horses. Do some quiet flatwork, such as walking, trotting, and a few circles in both directions. Usually one or two practice jumps are set up in the warmup ring (the ring outside the jumping ring). Just before your round, it is worth popping your horse over these once or twice. Never spend too much time on practice jumps and don't make them too high.

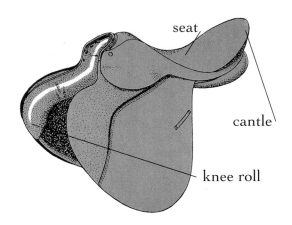

seat

cantle

knee roll

THE JUMP SADDLE

If you do a lot of show jumping, it might be worth buying a special jumping saddle. It is designed to be used with shorter stirrup leathers and has a forward-cut saddle flap. This often has extra padding, called a knee roll. The seat tends to be shallower and the cantle lower than on a general-purpose saddle. You will still need a general-purpose saddle for hacking and other riding.

Always Remember:

Pack your studs. You may need them to give your horse extra grip if the competition is in an outside arena. Pointed studs are used on hard ground. Square, chunky studs are used when it's muddy. As well as studs, you need a T-tap for cleaning the stud-hole in the shoe. You'll also need a wrench for tightening the stud, and petroleum jelly to lubricate the stud-hole before you put in the stud.

Don't forget to take out the studs as soon as the competition is over.

Petroleum jelly

Studs

T-tap

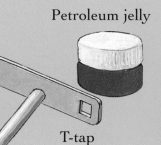

Evening
In a competition yesterday there was a jump with trays of water under the poles. There were yellow plastic ducks floating in them! Oscar stood and stared at them for ages— we ended up being eliminated.

Dressage

There is nothing mystical about dressage. It is just a way of training your horse or pony to carry out basic movements fluently, calmly, and obediently. Any type of horse will improve with schooling, and a well-schooled horse is a pleasure to ride.

K   E   H

A   C

The dressage arena
A standard arena is 131 by 66 ft (40 by 20 m) and you can mark it out on any flat ground. You can paint the letters on cones or old paint cans. Place them as shown here. The letters K, H, M, and F should be 20 ft (6 m) from the corners on the long sides. In a dressage test, the rider always enters at A. The center of the arena is known as X.

F   B   M

DRESSAGE SADDLE
This saddle isn't very comfortable for everyday riding, but it does get you into the correct position for dressage. It has a very deep seat and a straight-cut flap. The girth straps hanging below the panel show that it is meant to be used with a short girth. This stops the girth buckle from lying under your thigh.

CLOTHING FOR DRESSAGE
For dressage you should be clean and tidy, just as you are for showing. You should also wear gloves. Spurs and a whip are allowed. Your horse should also be well-groomed with its mane braided. Make sure your horse isn't wearing any boots, bandages, a saddle cloth, a colored browband, or anything else fancy. Don't be afraid to ask the organizer of a dressage competition if you are unsure of the dress rules.

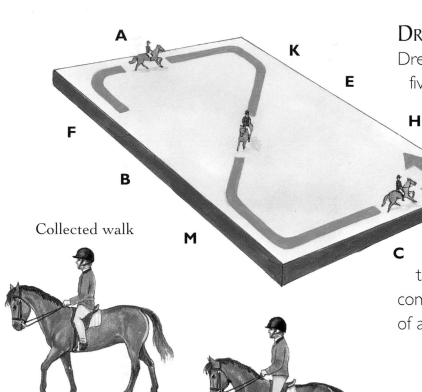

DRESSAGE TESTS

Dressage tests usually last about five minutes. They include different movements and paces for you and your horse to perform in a particular order. You have to do several changes of pace and direction. You can get a copy of the test from the event organizer. Dressage tests are specially written for dressage competitions and for the dressage section of a one-day event.

Collected walk

Working trot

Q How is dressage scored?

A All dressage tests are divided into sections. Each section contains one or more movements, such as a change of rein. You are given marks out of ten for each section. A score of five or more is a passing grade. These marks are recorded on your score sheet, along with any comments the judge makes. Marks are also given for the overall performance of both you and your horse. In a dressage competition, the competitor with the highest mark is the winner. In combined training (dressage and show jumping) and one-day events, the final mark is the number of penalties given. Penalties are given for any mistakes you make. So in these cases, the lower the score the better.

I got my first dressage score sheet back. It wasn't great, but the comments were very helpful. I'll do better next time.

Extended trot

Medium canter

DRESSAGE PACES

All of the movements that you do at junior level dressage are relatively easy for the average horse or pony. The paces are simply what you would normally do in basic schooling. When riding your test, try to concentrate on accuracy, smooth transitions from one gait to another, and getting your horse to bend when turning a circle. In many competitions you will be expected to perform the test from memory.

One-day event

My first one-day event was a DISASTER. I fell off on the cross-country course and then went on the wrong side of a flag!

This is a very popular event and is a true test of your horse's all-around ability. It combines the discipline of dressage, the stamina of cross-country jumping, and the accuracy and timing of the show-jumping ring. It is organized at all levels, from novice to experienced.

DRESSAGE
This is always the first of the three parts of a one-day event. The score that you get is the dressage penalty score. So you want it to be as low as possible.

SHOW JUMPING
This usually takes place after the cross-country. It is an ordinary show-jumping course. Any penalties that you get are added to the dressage score.

Stream

Tires

Finish

Tiger trap

Start

CHECKING THE COURSE
A map of the cross-country course is always displayed. Study it carefully before your turn. The time allowed to complete the course is also given, and you will get time penalties if you exceed it.

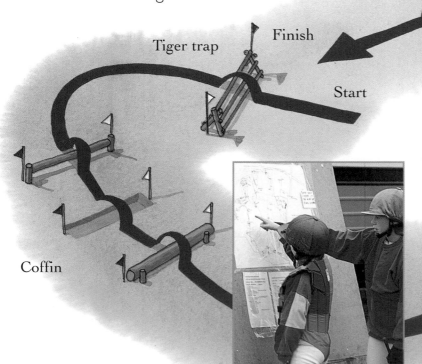

Coffin

V-shaped jump with alternative routes

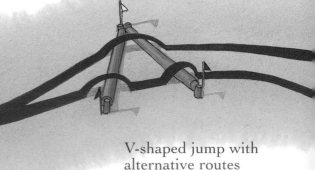

WATER JUMPS

Only experienced riders have to jump into or out of water, but you might be asked to splash through water and perhaps to jump a fence at the other side. If your horse hates water, some courses provide a learner fence to jump instead of going through the water.

BODY PROTECTORS

All cross-country riders should wear body protectors. These are specially designed, padded tabards that absorb shock and protect your spine, ribs, and shoulders. You should have your body protector properly fitted by a trained supplier.

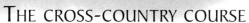

Straw bales

Bench or chair

Trakehner

THE CROSS-COUNTRY COURSE

Each jump is clearly numbered and is flagged with red and white flags. You ride between the flags. The red flag must be on your right and the white one on your left. Some jumps have more than one route. The shorter, direct route is often much more difficult.

Always Remember:

Plan the timing of your cross-country ride carefully. As you walk the course, note the places where you have to go slowly because of difficult ground. Just as importantly, note the places where you are able to speed up. This will help you to know where to make up some time if you feel that you are falling behind. Look carefully at each jump. In particular, decide which route you are going to take on those jumps that have more than one route. Does your horse like water? If not, then look to see whether or not there is a learner fence you can jump instead.

Puzzle with alternative routes

Transportation

Not many riders hack to shows because of the amount of traffic on the roads. Once you start competing regularly you will need to use a horse trailer. This gives you the chance to take part in different events over interesting and varied courses.

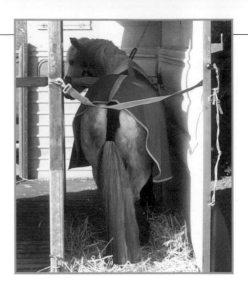

TRAVEL PROTECTION

Travel clothing guards against knocks and keeps your horse clean for the show. Horses usually wear traveling boots. These go from above the knee to just above the hoof. Your horse should also wear a lightweight rug, a tail bandage, and a tail guard. If your horse throws its head up a lot, it is a good idea for it to wear a poll guard on top of its head to prevent injury.

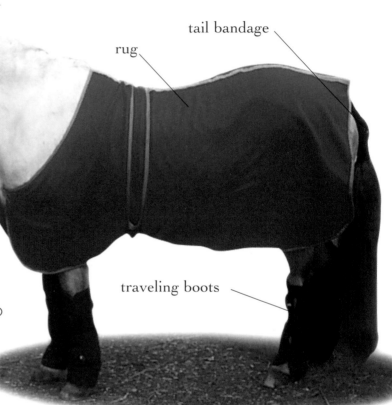

tail bandage

rug

traveling boots

4 pm—I think Oscar must have been fed in a trailer when he was young, because I never have any problem loading him. In fact, twice he has walked into the trailer on his own while I was talking to Annabel!

Always Remember:

Clean the trailer after you have used it. If the floor is wet, remove any straw and leave the ramps down so that air can circulate and allow the floor to dry. It is most important for your horse's safety that the floor should not rot. Cleaning and drying it should prevent this. Don't clean out your trailer while you are still at the show —it is very annoying for the owner of the field.

THE TRAILER

A two-horse trailer is the most popular kind of trailer as it lets your horse travel with a companion. Trailers with a front and a rear ramp are good, as your horse doesn't have to be backed out. This can make it less frightening for a nervous horse. Always load your horse by calmly walking in a straight line up the ramp. Tie up your horse with quite a short length of rope.

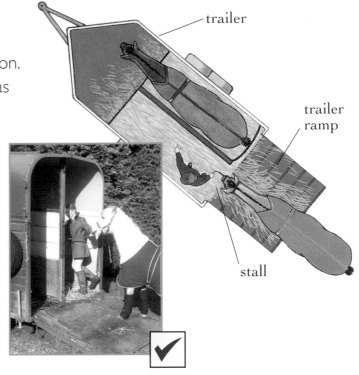

trailer

trailer ramp

stall

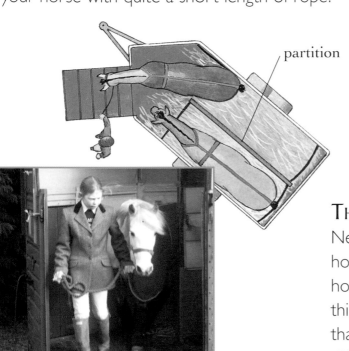

partition

THE WRONG WAY

Never try to load your horse as shown here. Your horse will win a battle like this because it is stronger than you. If your horse is difficult to load, ask an experienced person for help.

Q What do I need to know about hacking to a show?

A If the route is a safe one and you do not have big roads to cross or to ride along, hacking can be fun. Plan your route beforehand so that you know exactly which way to go. Take a head-collar with you, either on your horse or buckled around your waist. Allow plenty of time and enjoy the trip. It is best to travel with friends. At the showground, find a shady spot where you can tie up your horse. It helps if someone else can bring things like your grooming kit in the car.

Extra schooling

There is nothing like a competition for showing up basic problems, either yours or your horse's. Either way, there is only one solution—you both have to go back to school. If possible, get a good instructor to help you smooth out the rough patches.

LOSING

Losing is hard to take. The most important thing to do is to accept defeat gracefully. Go away, do some schooling, and come back to do your best at the next show. Remember that entering competitions is all about enjoying yourself. It isn't just the winning that is important.

GRID WORK

Getting back to basics is a good way to improve your chances at the next show. If your horse is rushing its jumps and not following your commands, however hard you try, you need to go back to the very beginning. Walk your horse calmly over poles on the ground. Then progress slowly to a grid of small jumps.

Make a video
One of the most helpful ways of improving your riding is to get a friend to videotape you during a schooling session. Until you see yourself riding, it can be difficult to tell just what you are doing wrong.

Don't try to advance too quickly, or all the old problems will come back. It is important to get your horse going steadily for you, answering to your legs and voice. Soon you will be able to complete a course of jumps without any problems.

BAD POSITION

It is important to keep a contact with your horse's mouth through the reins. This rider (near right) has reins that are too long. He has little control of his horse. The other rider (far right) is being left behind as the horse goes over the jump. Help your horse by sitting in the correct position and giving clear instructions.

Jumping too early

Oscar is turning into a really good jumper. I think he is enjoying it, because his ears always prick up when we enter the ring.

JUMPING PROBLEMS

Both the problems illustrated here show that you need to help your horse know when to take off. In the first, the horse has taken off too soon and will need to stretch out too far to clear the jump. In the second, a late takeoff means the horse knocks the jump down. With practice you can learn to recognize your horse's stride and when it should take off.

Jumping too late

FLATWORK

Flatwork is the most important part of training. By doing flatwork you will be able to do more exciting activities, like jumping, more efficiently, safely, and successfully. Try to spend a short time each day on schooling on the flat until your horse is moving out confidently. As you improve, gradually introduce more advanced movements. Make sure you keep having lessons with an experienced instructor.

Unusual activities

There are many different types of competition to enter and lots of ways to enjoy your horse. Here are some of the fun things that you can take part in. If you ask around, you may be able to join a group or club in your area.

Cross-country riding

Tuesday
Annabel and I had an invitation to learn all about tetrathlon. We were given a chance to shoot and shown exactly how to stand and hold the pistol. I completely missed the target with my first shot, but I soon learned not to wait too long before lining up and firing. I think it's another thing that you just get better and better at with practice!

TETRATHLON

This is a four-part event organized by the Pony Club. The competition usually takes place over two days. It creates a great feeling of team spirit and you are likely to make many friends. The four parts include riding over a cross-country course, shooting with a .177 air pistol, cross-country running over a certain distance, and swimming as far as you can in a certain number of minutes. The older you are, the further or longer the races will be. Usually, the shooting and swimming take place on the first day and riding and running are held on the second. The points you get for each event are added together to determine the winner.

Race information
- Riding — 1-1^{1}/2 mi (1,600-2,500 m) cross-country
- Running — 1,100-3,300 yards (1,000-3,000 m)
- Swimming — points are scored for every length you swim for 2-3 minutes
- Shooting — 10 shots at two targets from 23-33 ft (7-10 m)

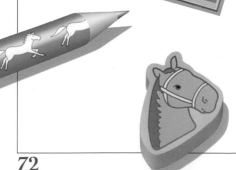

roping horn

Western bridle

long leather stirrups

WESTERN RIDING

Western riders use a specially designed saddle and bridle. A Western saddle has a roping horn, a high cantle, and long leather stirrups. It is heavier than an ordinary saddle and the horse is gradually introduced to it. You sit deep in the saddle and ride with long stirrup leathers. This allows you to sit in the saddle for a long time without getting too tired. This is useful for cowboys who spend many hours in the saddle. You hold the reins with one hand and use neck-reining to steer the horse.

Lunchtime I thought I might take up endurance riding and went for a really long three-hour ride. Oscar was fine when we got back, but I was so exhausted I could hardly stand. Perhaps endurance riding can wait!

ENDURANCE RIDING

Endurance riding is competing over long distances to be completed as efficiently as possible without distress to your horse. At various points along the route, your horse is examined by a veterinarian before you're allowed to continue. You are also met by an assistant who gives you and your horse whatever help or refreshment you need.

Q What is the difference between the tetrathlon and the modern pentathlon?

A The modern pentathlon consists of riding, shooting, running, swimming, and fencing. Tetrathlon doesn't include fencing. Most pentathletes start their career in the Pony Club and then take up fencing as they get older. Riding in modern pentathlon is different from tetrathlon because the competitors ride horses that they have never seen before. The riding is usually over a show-jumping course. In tetrathlon, you ride your own horse and you don't do any show jumping. In ordinary athletics, the pentathlon comprises various field and track events and dates back to as long ago as 708 B.C.

CHAPTER 4
The world of horses

Different types of horse have been bred for different uses. Today, the tiny Shetland pony and the huge workhorse look very different, yet they both have a common ancestor.

RUSSIAN GOLDEN HORSE
The narrow Russian horse, the Akhal-Teke, is known as the "golden horse." This is because it has a bright, metallic golden sheen on its coat. Originally a desert horse, it is thought to be an ancestor of the Arabian. It has great speed and stamina.

ARABIAN
Perhaps the most beautiful horse of all time, the Arabian is noted for its concave face, glorious head, and high tail carriage. It displays amazing stamina and extreme hardiness. It is a native of the Middle East and is used for all types of work from riding and racing, to pulling carts and carrying produce. The true Arabian is not very big. It stands at between only 14.2 and 15 hands high (57 to 60 inches), but it is a unique horse.

Morning
I wish I knew exactly what breed of pony Oscar is. I expect he's a crossbreed, but he doesn't have a pedigree so I can't be sure.

Did you know?
There are about 300 different horse and pony breeds in the world. They range from the heavy horses of northern Europe to the tiny Falabella pony of South America. One original wild horse, the Tarpan, still exists in captivity. But Przewalski's horse, discovered in Mongolia in the 1920s, is now thought to be extinct. Both of these original wild horses display a coarse, heavy head, a stand-up mane, and a dorsal stripe.

HANOVERIAN

Originally bred in Germany, the Hanoverian was used for riding and farmwork. It was later crossed with thoroughbreds to produce a well-built riding horse. Many leading European riders ride Hanoverians, and these horses are very much in demand for show jumping.

IRISH HUNTER

The Irish hunter is not a breed but a type. Ireland produces some of the finest horses in the world. The Irish draft horse is a strong, well-built working horse. As horses were used less in agriculture, the Irish draft was crossed with the thoroughbred to produce a riding horse. This was then bred with Connemara horses to become the popular Irish hunter.

Thursday
I am keeping a scrapbook of all the horse breeds of the world —with a difference. I can put a picture of any breed in, but only if I have actually seen it. So my book isn't coming along very fast! I told Mom that a tour of Russia would be a good idea, followed by a trip around Scandinavia, but you can guess what she said.

Shetland pony
Scotland

NATIVE PONIES

Of all the regions in the world, the British Isles have the largest number of different breeds of native pony—nine in total. The New Forest and Welsh ponies are ideal for children to ride. Scandinavia and Iceland also have small, hardy native ponies, all of them strong enough to carry grown-ups.

Q Are horse fairs still held?

A Horse fairs—places where horses and ponies are bought and sold—still exist, such as Golega Fair in Portugal, below. In England, one of the best known is the Stow Fair in Gloucestershire, where young ponies can be bought quite cheaply. The pony breed societies hold annual sales of yearlings that can be trained to become good riding ponies. The sales help control the numbers of wild ponies roaming their natural habitat.

New Forest pony
England

Exmoor pony
England

Across continents

Sunday
There are two kinds of pinto horses, the Ovaro and the Tobiano. The Ovaro is dark with patches of white over it. The Tobiano has a white coat with large patches of dark color. Pintos were popular with Native Americans and cowboys.

Today, wherever you go in the world, the primary use of horses and ponies is for recreation. In some poor countries the horse still fills its traditional role—that of helping its master to make a living. But the bond between horse and master may still be very close.

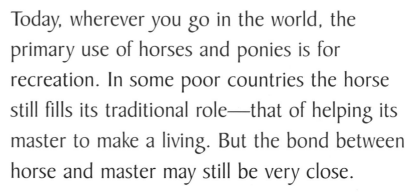

SOUTH AMERICA

This is the home of horses descended from Spanish horses imported nearly 500 years ago. The Argentinians ride Criollos. These are short, stocky horses that are well suited to herding cattle. Criollos are crossed with thoroughbreds to make very good polo ponies. Argentina is also home to the smallest pony in the world—the Falabella. This tiny pony stands at less than 7 hands (28 inches) high.

ASIA

Remains of prehistoric horses have been found in India, and horses are said to have been introduced into China 4,000 years ago. The Chinese pony is very similar to the Mongolian pony, which resembles the early Tarpan horse (page 74).

Waler
Australia

AUSTRALIA

There are no horses native to Australia. The Waler, now an Australian breed, is descended from horses brought by settlers in the 1700s. Brumbies, wild horses living in the outback, come from horses turned loose in the gold rushes of the 1800s.

CONQUISTADORS

The Spanish who discovered and conquered the New World, the conquistadors, brought their horses with them. These caused as much interest, awe, and excitement among the Native Americans as did the arrival of the white men themselves. Until this time, the American continent had no horses at all. Some escaped into the wild, and were the ancestors of the wild horses of the plains.

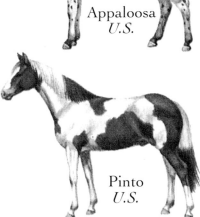

Appaloosa
U.S.

NORTH AMERICAN HORSES

The American quarter horse, with its short bursts of speed and ability to turn and twist, is ideally suited to cattle-herding. The remarkable Tennessee walking horse, with its amazingly comfortable running gait, suited the plantation owner's need to spend all day in the saddle without getting tired.

Pinto
U.S.

Tennessee walking horse
U.S.

MUSTANGS

The wild horse of America, the mustang, is a direct descendant of the horses that came over with the Spanish conquistadors. Big herds of these horses used to roam the plains of the central U.S., but they were long considered worthless. So, fifty years ago, a registry of Spanish mustang horses was established with the aim of preserving their best characteristics —hardiness, intelligence, and stamina.

The Western horse

In the American West, the horse had a particular function—herding cattle across the vast plains of the continent and carrying its rider many miles a day. No wonder that the Western horse displays special characteristics and wears a saddle and bridle well suited to its role in life.

Later—I'm in big trouble. I took Oscar's noseband off to turn him into a cowboy horse and now I've lost it. I was sure I'd left it in the tack room. Now I've got to use my allowance to buy a new one. Still, he really looked like a Western horse!

RODEO
Rodeo competitions provided cowboys with a chance to show off their riding and cattle skills. Today they are a popular attraction in the American West. They offer prizes to riders who can stay on a bucking horse the longest, rope a calf the quickest, and ride a bull without falling off.

JUNIOR RODEO RIDERS
America has an association of young rodeo riders. Their ages range from under-8 to 19, and they compete at all sorts of cowboy contests. Rodeos include goat tying, calf roping, steer wrestling and riding, bareback riding, and bronco riding.

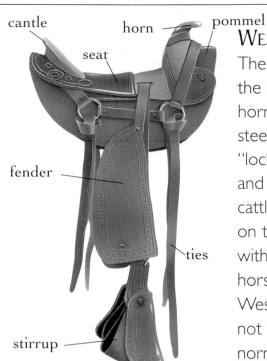

cantle · horn · pommel · seat · fender · ties · stirrup

WESTERN SADDLE AND BRIDLE

The seat of the Western saddle is deep, for the comfort of the rider on a long ride. The horn is for attaching a rope when roping steers. The cantle and pommel are high to "lock" the rider in position when twisting and turning during the process of herding cattle. The Western bridle has long shanks on the bit that are used in conjunction with a leather curb strap to act on the horse's poll (the part of the head between the ears). Western bridles don't have a noseband. Split reins—reins not buckled together—are popular. One-handed riding is normal, so cowboys steer their horses using neck-reining.

MYTHS AND MODERN WAYS

Cowboys did spend many hours in the saddle and they slept under the stars. But they did not ride the huge horses that you see in Western films. Real cowboys preferred small horses, often ponies, and usually rode more than one a day. Cowboys sometimes changed mounts six times a day. Today, cowboys are more likely to be seen on dirt bikes or at rodeos than out on a horse.

Annabel and I tried roping a fence post, and the loop never came near enough. Just imagine trying it with a moving steer!

WESTERN TRAILS

The modern-day rider can enjoy a great vacation at a Western ranch catering to tourists, riding out on the old cowboy trails. Trail rides can be just one day or you can go on longer rides lasting several days. Accommodation usually involves camping out at night and cooking your own food on an open fire. Trail riding is enjoyed by many people.

Racehorses

From the time when horses were first domesticated, riders have tried to outdo each other. Racing has existed as an organized sport for about 400 years. Today it is done worldwide. The best horses are greatly admired and can be worth a great deal of money.

THOROUGHBRED
The thoroughbred is the fastest horse in the world. It is descended from one of three Arabian stallions, the Darley Arabian, the Byerley Turk, and the Godolphin Barb. Every racehorse entered in the General Stud Book has at least one in its pedigree. The thoroughbred develops early. This is why two-year-olds can be ridden and raced. Every thoroughbred's official birthday is January 1st.

WHERE IT ALL BEGAN
The ancient Greeks enjoyed public racing, but in much of Europe for the next thousand years or so, racing was mainly private. In the late 1600s, it became more formalized in England, and other countries soon followed suit. The Jockey Club was created to oversee the sport.

STEEPLECHASING
Racing over jumps used to be held between two landmarks, often the steeples of churches (hence steeplechasing). The world's most famous race over jumps—the Grand National—began in 1839. Most horses in jump racing today start by racing on the flat. Too slow for flat racing, they are tried over hurdles, then over jumps. If the longer distance suits them, they can race for many more years.

RACING AROUND THE WORLD

There are several great races. Among the most famous are the English Derby, the American Kentucky Derby, the Australian Melbourne Cup, and the French Prix de l'Arc de Triomphe. Race meetings are held all over the world and provide a focal point of interest for local people. Hong Kong's racetrack, Happy Valley, is set in the middle of the crowded city.

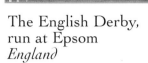

The English Derby, run at Epsom
England

Happy Valley Racetrack
Hong Kong

The Kentucky Derby, Churchill Downs, *Kentucky*

Friday
I really would like to be a jockey. Girls and boys can be apprenticed to racehorse trainers now. But Dad says it's a hard life and only the very best can get to the top. Perhaps, one day, I could be the very first girl to win the Kentucky Derby!

TROTTERS

Harness-racing is popular in America and France. The horses have been trained to move at an amazingly swift trot instead of a gallop. Their other artificial gait, the pace, is where the legs on the same side move forward at the same time. These two gaits ensure the horse pulls the two-wheeled, lightweight sulky very smoothly.

Riding styles

Through the ages, most riding styles have changed. A few have stayed much the same as always. Others have been affected by clothing styles, social attitudes, or improvements in technique. In some cases, the interest of modern-day enthusiasts keeps an older riding style going.

3 pm—I tried riding like a medieval knight on Oscar the other day. They used to ride with really long stirrups. It wasn't very easy, especially when it came to rising trot. It's almost impossible to stand up in the stirrups when your legs are straight to start with.

Racing

An American jockey named Tod Sloan changed the style of race-riding forever in the 1800s. Before he came to England to ride in races, jockeys rode with long stirrups. Tod introduced the very short stirrup leather. He was laughed at and called a "monkey on a stick." Despite this, his technique was soon copied by jockeys everywhere.

Did you know?

The Spanish Riding School in Vienna trains its horses in what is called the classic style of horsemanship. The beautiful white Lipizzaner stallions are taught High School movements (right). The Spanish Riding School travels all over the world giving demonstrations, which are well worth a visit. The horses are very supple, calm, and obedient, and wonderfully in tune with their talented riders.

JUMPING

Everyone today is taught the forward seat when jumping. This lets the hands follow the movement of the horse and keeps the rider's weight evenly distributed. This method is one hundred years old. It dates back to the teachings of an Italian cavalry officer, Federico Caprilli. Before that, riders leaned forward on takeoff and back on landing.

WESTERN

With a deep seat and straight legs, cowboys found that they could ride for many miles and not get too tired. Provided that the saddle fits properly, this style is kind to the horse, too. Western horses are trained to respond to the reins touching the neck. A touch on the right side makes the horse turn left and vice versa.

SIDESADDLE

Sidesaddle riding is considered a very elegant riding style. In the past it was the only acceptable way for a lady to ride. The "leaping head," the downturned horn fitted below the upward horn on the saddle, makes it possible for sidesaddle riders to have a firm seat, jump, and gallop safely.

MEDIEVAL KNIGHTS

The cavalry was an important part of the army, and all officers were mounted. They rode with long stirrups, straight legs, and their feet forward. This style looks similar to that of Western riders. The armor worn by the military horsemen of northern Europe was so bulky that only very strong horses could carry them. Some needed cranes to lift them onto their horses. If a soldier fell off, he was not able to get on again.

Horses in fiction

Stories about horses have been popular for many years, from the classics of earlier days to the pony books of today. Some fictional horses live forever, continuing to delight each generation of readers. Some of them are listed here.

Tuesday
Before I had Oscar, I spent most of my time reading. I thought I'd read all the horse books ever written! But Oscar takes up so much of my day, reading has moved into second place. Now, most of my books are practical ones on horse care.

SILVER

This horse was almost certainly the first to become famous through radio and television. He is a handsome gray who belongs to the Lone Ranger. The Lone Ranger is a masked man who rides anonymously through the Wild West, solving crimes and restoring law and order wherever he goes.

FLICKA

Flicka is the horse heroine of *My Friend Flicka*, a book written by Mary O'Hara about the love of a boy for his horse. The setting is a ranch in Wyoming, and the book gives a vivid picture of domesticating and training wild horses in the West just before World War II. The picture (left) is from the movie based on the book. The book is no longer in print, but it can be found in second-hand bookstores.

BLACK BEAUTY

A young writer, Anna Sewell, hated seeing carriage horses in bearing reins. These are straps that forced horses to carry their heads at an uncomfortable angle. She wrote a book about the life of a carriage horse, *Black Beauty*. She included other characters, such as Merrylegs and Ginger. The book is a classic and led to the prohibition of bearing reins in the U.K.

THE RED PONY

The Red Pony is a short story by John Steinbeck. The pony, which belongs to a young boy, gets sick and dies. The boy blames his father for the pony's death, but the two of them struggle to build a new relationship. In 1949, the story, which does finally have a happy ending, was made into a prize-winning film.

ROSINANTE

This horse is an example of beauty being in the eye of the beholder. Rosinante is an ugly old nag who generally fails in anything he is asked to do. But to his owner, Don Quixote, a self-styled knight, he is a status symbol and the best horse in the world. *Don Quixote* was written by Miguel de Cervantes in the 1600s and is a classic of European literature.

Afternoon—Annabel and I go to our local library, but we can't always find the books we want to read. So Annabel said why don't we get together with friends at the stable and form our own book-lending group. I thought that was a brilliant idea. So that's what we've done. There are loads of books I haven't read yet.

In the beginning

Early horses looked nothing like the horses of today. It took 50 million years of evolution for the cat-sized creature that lived in the Northern Hemisphere to become the handsome, elegant horse we all admire now. Only in the last 5,000 years has the horse been ridden by man.

HYRACOTHERIUM

Also known as Eohippus ("Dawn Horse"), Hyracotherium was a funny little creature. It had four toes on its front feet and three toes on the back. From all the fossilized bones found in the southern U.S., it seems likely that it originated on the American continent.

Hyracotherium

MESOHIPPUS

The next stage in the evolution was the Mesohippus. It had a similar bone structure to the Hyracotherium, but was bigger. Still a small creature, it was beginning to emerge from the forest to graze on the plains. Its feet were still multitoed, but the outer toes were less pronounced. Its weight was carried on the central toe.

Mesohippus

INTO DANGER

The little prehistoric horses, coming out of the safety of the forest, were able to run quite fast. This was their way of avoiding danger. But they were no match for predatory birds. These creatures, with their sharp eyesight, could easily spot the tiny horses, in spite of their striped camouflage. Many horses ended up as a tasty morsel.

Q How big were the first horses?

A They were very small. Hyracotherium was not much bigger than a domestic cat. Certainly too small for a human to ride, even if early man had been in existence at the time. Throughout the millions of years of evolution, horses got bigger and stronger.

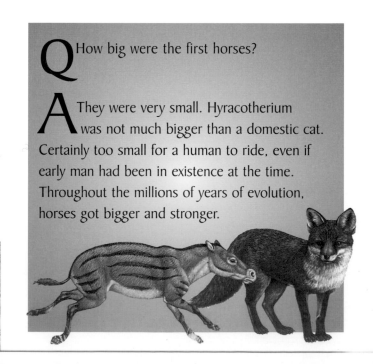

HOTBLOODS AND COLDBLOODS

As the horse evolved, two types emerged. In the northern countries, the coldbloods were predominant. They developed into the heavy horses of today, powerfully built, strong creatures. They could be trained to pull a plow or wagon or to carry a man in a full suit of armor. Farther south were the hotbloods, horses like the desert Arabian. These were lighter in build but very hardy and tough. Many of today's horses are crosses between the two types and are known as warmbloods.

EQUUS

This is the true horse, common ancestor of all our present-day horses. It was a single-toed mammal standing about 13 hands high (52 inches). Equus had a large head, heavy neck, faint stripes on its fore- and hindquarters, and possibly a dorsal stripe along its backbone. Its mane was short and stood up like a shaving brush.

Merichippus

Equus

MERICHIPPUS

Merichippus was more recognizable as a horse. The outer toes had almost disappeared and the central toe was broadening into a hoof. This was a creature of the plains, no longer feeding on trees but capable of eating grass. Its natural defense was to run away. In spite of the vast prairies of America, horses disappeared from the American continent. They did not return for several thousand years, until brought back by the conquistadors in the 1500s.

Morning
I had a nightmare last night. I dreamed that I was a Dawn Horse living in a prehistoric world. I was being chased by a caveman. I was so glad to wake up!

Heavy horses

In their time, the size and strength of heavy horses made them the most important of the horse breeds, and even today they are impressive. But in many places they no longer have a role, and only careful conservation will prevent them from dying out.

OLD AMERICAN HORSES

The most versatile all-purpose horse in America is the Morgan. It is a combination of the best qualities of both draft and riding horses. It is powerful, intelligent, and has great stamina.

PLOWING WITH HORSES

Until 50 years ago, heavy horses were used for farmwork throughout the Western world. They are still used in some countries. These massive but willing animals were the engines of agriculture. They can pull plows and threshing machines, and work tirelessly all day.

JOUSTING

A man in full armor is very heavy, and the horse had to be immensely strong to carry him. During the Age of Chivalry, tournaments became popular. Knights competed against each other, trying to knock each other off their horses. The two riders used their lances as battering rams.

TODAY'S CAVALRY

Heavy horses are no longer used by the cavalry, which does not need weight-carriers. The cavalry has no role in modern warfare, but it is still an impressive sight when taking part in state ceremonies. The annual Trooping of the Color on Horseguards Parade in London is a spectacular sight.

DRAY HORSES

In Britain, several big breweries still use heavy horses to pull their drays. It is not unusual to see beer barrels being unloaded outside a pub (bar), while the pair of shire horses harnessed to the dray enjoy their lunch

from nosebags. Classes for tradesmen's drays are usually held at agricultural shows. They parade around the arena giving a magnificent display.

Suffolk Punch
England

Clydesdale
Scotland

Dutch Draft
Holland

HEAVY HORSES TODAY

Efforts are now being made to conserve breeds that might otherwise die out. The Suffolk Punch, a British breed that is always chestnut and has no feathers (longer hair) on its legs, is the most endangered. Special societies support the preservation of working breeds around the world.

Working with horses

If you love riding and horses, it is not surprising that you would like to go on being with horses. You may choose to go on riding in your leisure time, on weekends, or in vacations. Or you may, like many others before you, decide to work with horses full time.

TEACHING

Firstly, you need to be a proficient rider. Secondly, it's important that you enjoy people as well as horses. Today, instructors have formal qualifications, which you should study for if you want to teach. The American Riding Instructors Association has a course of examinations that you can take to become a riding instructor.

Did you know?

To become a farrier you must enroll on a two-week basic farrier course where you learn to make shoes, basic trimming, and shoeing techniques. Or you can enroll on longer courses that include therapeutic and corrective shoeing. There are a number of farriery schools in the U.S. Following this, you can take up an apprenticeship with a "Journeyman Farrier." Here you will gain a lot of experience until you are ready to try it alone.

Afternoon—Oscar really enjoys lots of company, especially with people. I think he would like to have a job where he could be with humans. He would work on his laptop when he was traveling on the train to his office each day. Imagine that?!

BARN WORKER/STABLE HELP

A barn worker's job can be very rewarding although it is hard work and the pay is quite poor. You will be expected to feed the horses, clean the stalls, repair fencing, help out when the farrier comes, and generally keep the barn clean and tidy.

RACING

Jockeys are very small and light. To be an apprentice jockey, you must not be heavier than 110 pounds (50 kg). Apprenticeships can be had with stables all over the world. Apprentices are trained in horse handling, grooming, hoof care, horse health, feeding, stable skills, and trackwork riding. If you are too heavy to become a jockey, you could consider becoming a barn worker at a racing stable.

BARN MANAGER

Barn managers are responsible for the day-to-day running of the barn and also for the barn workers and the horses. Although a degree isn't essential, it is helpful to have a degree in Equine Studies or Equine Management. This will ensure you have all the necessary skills, such as equine business knowledge, communications skills, riding, and horsecare skills.

Tuesday
I think it would be good fun to be a barn manager. Just think, you'd get to spend every day with loads of different horses. Mom says it's hard work and a really responsible job, but I reckon I could do it. I'll just have to get some more practical horsecare skills and then do a training course. How hard can it be?! I think it would be worth it.

Q What about helping out with riding for the handicapped?

A Every year around 20,000 people volunteer to help out at North American Riding for the Handicapped Association (NARHA) centers. If you have no horsemanship experience, you will need to be over 14 years old. If you are younger and have some experience, it is likely that you'll be accepted. Volunteers help by leading the horse, sidewalking (walking alongside the horse to help support the rider), grooming, tacking up horses, cooling off horses, cleaning tack, helping with fundraisers, and assisting with administrative duties.

Quiz time

It's surprising how much you learn when you are doing things every day. Try the Quiz—and get your friends to try, too—and see what you can remember.

Always Remember:
Keep taking lessons. Even the most experienced riders continue having lessons. With a good instructor, you can make sure you don't get into bad habits. If your horse is refusing to do what you want, check that its tack fits well, that you are feeding it the right food, and that it hasn't injured itself. By taking care of your horse, you will have more fun together.

1 What are the natural aids?

2 What are the artificial aids?

3 Name four types of bedding.

4 What name is given to each of the following?
- *a* A steeply sloping rump
- *b* A soft swelling just above the fetlock
- *c* A bony swelling below the knee

5 When cantering in a circle, which leg should a horse always lead with?

6 What is useful for making your horse's white socks look whiter?

7 Why is neck-reining useful in gymkhana games?

8 Starting with A and moving clockwise around the arena, write down the letters in their correct order.

9 Who was the first jockey to ride with very short stirrups?

10 Where do the "golden" horses come from?

Useful addresses

U.S.A. Pony Clubs
4041 Iron Works
   Parkway
Lexington, KY 40511-8462
www.ponyclub.org
Tel: (859) 254-7669

U.S.A. Equestrian, Inc.
4047 Iron Works
   Parkway
Lexington, KY 40511-8463
www.equestrian.org
Tel: (859) 254-2476

Monday
Annabel and I did a quiz on Saturday. Loads of them were about horses, and we got every one right. Cool!

Answers
1 Legs, hands, body, voice. 2 Whip, martingale, spurs. 3 Straw, shavings, sawdust, shredded paper. 4 *a* Goose rump *b* Windgall *c* Splint. 5 The inside leg. 6 Chalk. 7 It leaves you one hand free for holding equipment. 8 A, K, E, H, C, M, B, F. 9 Tod Sloan. 10 Russia.

Glossary

aids
The means by which a rider communicates with a horse. These can be natural or artificial.

bars
Ridges underneath the hoof on either side of the frog.

bit
A metal bar attached to the reins that fits in the pony's mouth.

cantle
The highest part of the saddle at the back.

changing the rein
Changing the direction in which you ride around the ring (arena).

class
Each show is split into classes. You choose which classes to enter. Different classes are designed for different abilities and age groups.

clenches
Horseshoe nails after they have passed through the hoof and the tops of them have been twisted off.

contact
The link, through the reins, between a horse's mouth and a rider's hands.

dock
The area under a horse's tail.

dressage
Exercises performed on flat ground to show the obedience, agility, and suppleness of a horse.

farrier
A trained person who takes care of a horse's feet and fits new shoes.

fetlock joints
The joint that sticks out just above the hoof.

frog
The V-shaped part of the underneath of the hoof. It absorbs shock.

gaits
The movements made naturally by a horse—the walk, trot, canter, and gallop.

gelding
A male horse or pony that is suitable for riding. A female is called a mare.

girth
The wide strap that holds the saddle on.

hack
A ride out on a horse or pony.

hackamore
A bridle that has no bit. The horse is controlled by pressure exerted on its nose.

hands
Horses and ponies are measured in hands. One hand is equal to 4 inches (10 cm).

hunter trials
Cross-country competition.

laminitis
Sore feet, usually caused by overeating.

Glossary

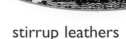

livery
The name given to the practice of keeping a horse at a stall that isn't your own.

martingale
The straps that stop a horse from putting its head too high in the air for the rider to be able to have any control.

napping
Describes a horse being stubborn and refusing to go in the right direction.

neat's-foot oil
Substance that can be painted onto leather to keep it supple.

neck-reining
Guiding a horse with only one hand on the reins.

poll guard
A covering that protects the part of a horse's head between its ears.

pommel
The front part of the saddle.

rasping
When a vet removes sharp edges from the teeth of a horse.

refusal
When a pony stops in front of a jump instead of jumping over it.

salute
Gesture made by a rider to tell the judge that they have finished their display.

schedule
List of classes in a show or cross-country event.

seat
The position in which you sit in the saddle. You should be able to draw a vertical line through your ear, shoulder, hip, and heel when your position is correct.

stirrup irons
The two metal loops attached to the stirrup leathers that a rider's feet go in.

stirrup leathers
The straps that hold the stirrup irons onto the saddle.

studs
Metal bolts that screw into a horse's shoes to give it extra grip on slippery ground.

suspension (moment of)
When all four of the horse's feet are off the ground.

transition
The change from one gait to another.

traveling boots
Padded leggings that stretch from above the knee to the hoof, used when traveling.

vaulting
1) Gymnastics on horseback
2) Leaping onto a horse.

vetting
When a vet checks the health of a horse or pony.

withers
The projecting bone at the base of the neck.

yearling
A horse that is between one and two years old.

Index

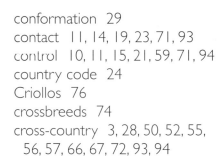

mane 38, 39, 46, 48, 52, 53, 57, 64, 74, 87
mare 93
martingale 14, 15, 61, 94
Merichippus 87
Mesohippus 86
Morgan 88
mustangs 77

napping 94
native ponies 75
neat's-foot oil 57, 94
neck-reining 59, 73, 79, 92, 94
neck strap 22, 23
noseband 21, 41, 78, 79

one-day events 50, 65, 66-67

pentathlon 73
pintos 76, 77
poisonous plants 32, 33
poles 21, 22, 23, 55, 70
poll 79
poll guard 49, 68, 94
pommel 10, 11, 79, 94
Przewalski's horse 74

racehorses 80-81
rasping 47, 94
refusal 23, 51, 94
reins 9, 10, 11, 13, 14, 18, 19, 23, 26, 41, 59, 60, 61, 70, 71, 73, 79, 83, 93, 94
riding boots 8, 9, 53, 60, 61
riding coat 8, 9
riding hat 8, 9, 13, 37, 53, 60
riding schools 4, 15
riding stables 5, 30, 31, 36, 37, 48, 53, 56, 57, 70, 91

roads 26-27, 28, 45, 68, 69
rodeo 78, 79
rump 7, 12, 13, 29, 92
Russian golden horse 74, 92

saddle 10, 11, 14, 16, 17, 18, 19, 21, 23, 25, 27, 37, 40, 46, 55, 56, 57, 59, 61, 63, 73, 77, 78, 79, 83, 93, 94
saddle cloth 40

salute 60, 94
schedule 50, 51, 61, 94
scoring 65, 66
seat 5, 10, 23, 83, 94
security 35, 37
shelter 35
show jumping 3, 54, 61, 62-63, 65, 66, 73, 75
show ring 22, 54, 55, 60-61, 62, 63, 71, 93
sidesaddle 83
socks 52, 92
Spanish Riding School 82
splints 29
spurs 14, 15, 64
stall 30, 31, 36, 38, 90, 94
steeplechasing 80
stirrup bar 10

stirrup irons 10, 40, 94
stirrup leathers 10, 11, 19, 41, 63, 73, 82, 94
stirrups 9, 11, 12, 13, 17, 19, 23, 25, 59, 73, 82, 83, 92
studs 45, 56, 63, 94
Suffolk Punch 89
suspension (moment of) 94

tack 28, 37, 40-41, 46, 53, 55, 57, 61, 92
tail 6, 29, 39, 46, 49, 52, 53, 57, 93
tail bandage 49, 68
tail guard 49, 57, 68
Tarpan 74, 76
teeth 47, 94
Tennessee walking horse 77
tetrathlon 72, 73
thoroughbreds 75, 76, 80
training 5, 20, 21, 25, 64, 71
longe training 21
transition 18, 19, 65, 94
transportation 4, 68-69
turning 14, 26, 27, 83

vaccination 47
vaulting 11, 59, 94
veterinarian 28, 46, 47, 57, 73, 94
vetting 28, 94

Waler 76
warmbloods 87
warming up 61, 63
warmup ring 54, 63
water
(drinking) 34, 35, 43, 47, 56, 57
(jumping over) 50, 51, 63, 67
Western riding 73, 78, 79, 83
whip 11, 14, 15, 64
withers 40, 59, 94

yearling 75, 94